RSPB
BIRD
LIFE
annual

Compiled by Linda Bennett

PURNELL

Contents

Male redstart

Peter Holden, who leads the RSPB's Young Ornithologists' Club (YOC for short) says "You too can help us in the vital campaign to protect and conserve wildlife."
The YOC is for young people under 15 who are particularly interested in wild birds. It encourages people not just to watch birds but to study them. YOC members are detectives, finding out more about the world of birds each day.

But the work of the club does not stop there. If you are a YOC member, you will always be busy with conservation work. National projects are organised, with which you can help scientists by carrying out simple but important research. Special holiday courses are held all over Britain—some of which combine birdwatching with canoeing, sailing, pony trekking, mountaincraft or fishing. And regular outings are arranged to RSPB reserves; there are more than 50 throughout the country.

Every two months you will receive a special, full-colour club magazine, *Bird Life*, to keep you informed of all these events. Packed with interesting articles, this magazine is a must for any young person interested in birds.

The YOC has a small subscription—only £1.25 for an individual member. Brothers and sisters can join together for only £1.55, sharing one copy of the magazine. Many schools have their own groups. Perhaps there is one at your school?

Join now by writing for an application form from YOC, The Lodge, Sandy, Bedfordshire, SG19 2DL.

Young long-eared owls

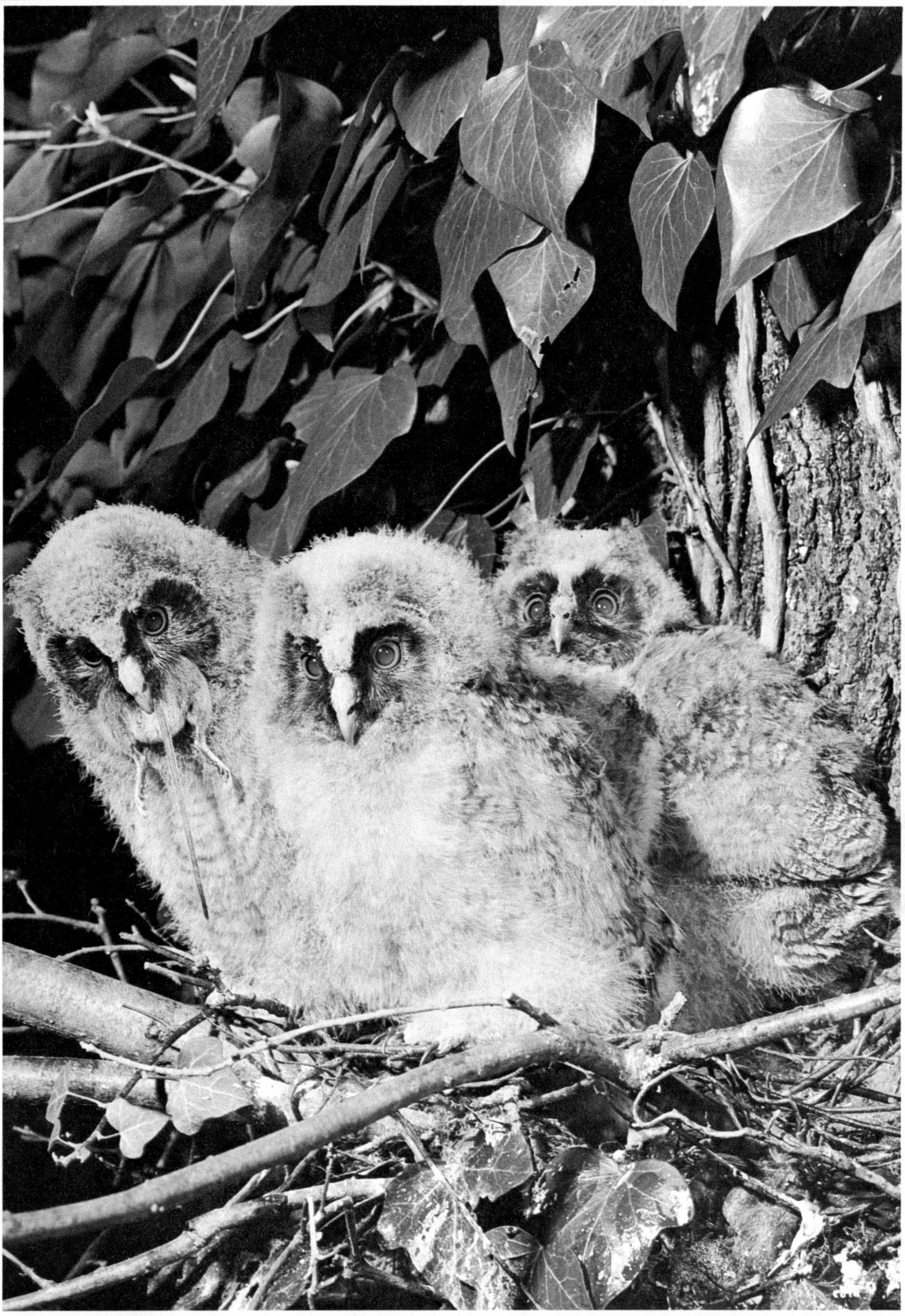

BIRD

Where to start

Houses and sheds make excellent hides where you can watch birds without them seeing or being afraid of you. If you do not know of a suitable outbuilding you can easily make your own shelter in a quiet corner of the garden.

There are always different species to be seen from the windows of your home. Make a check-list for each window and see whether the species and numbers of birds vary. If you live in a flat, many of the birds you see will be flying. It takes practice and patience to recognise a bird in flight. However, if you hang a peanut holder from one of the windows, tits and sparrows will come to feed, and you will be able to see them at close quarters.

If you are lucky enough to have a garden, keep a list of the regular visitors, the regular feeders and those which fly over the garden but do not come down and settle—these might be swifts or gulls.

You can also encourage birds to feed in your garden. The article **Make your garden a bird reserve** on page 22 tells you how to do this.

The next step

Once you have mastered the common birds in your garden, it is time to go further afield. Visit your nearest stretch of water or local

Before sorting out all the problems of birdwatching, let us answer one question—"Why watch birds at all?" People have a natural curiosity about the world in which they live, in particular about all the living things which form a large part of it. Birds are large and colourful, they can be seen in any part of the country and at any time of the year. They are full of movement and are often present in large numbers and in great variety. No other group of animals possesses all these qualities. Wherever you may be, if you are interested in birds, you will always be busy.

WATCHING

how when and where

park. Here the main problem is getting close enough to the birds in order to see them clearly.

Often, it is by far the best to remain still and quiet, and wait for the bird to come to you. A small bird feeding in a hedge will generally move slowly along its length. So, if you sit a little way in front of the bird, it will probably come very near to you. Small birds have difficulty in recognizing large, stationary objects when they are very close to them. As long as you remain perfectly still, the birds behave normally, without showing any signs of fear.

If the birds will not come to you, then you must go to them; this involves movement, which immediately makes you visible and may cause alarm. When approaching a bird, use what cover is available. Try to keep a hedge, bank or tree trunk between yourself and the bird. If you cannot move behind these barriers then walk directly in front, so you are against a dark background and not outlined

against the sky. If you have to, cross any open ground very slowly, even get down and crawl on your hands and knees. It is also a good idea not to walk straight toward a bird but to pass on one side as if you have not seen it. Passers-by who are not looking out for birds often get much closer than the bird-watcher who is obviously stalking them!

If you are walking over ground covered with leaves and twigs and cannot move quietly, approach down-wind so any noise that you make will be carried away. It is also best to move towards birds with the sun behind you, then you are in the shadow, but the birds are in the sunlight and their colours are more easily seen.

The only way to watch birds at the sea or on a lake is to sit on the shore or landing-stage and hope that they will come in close. Here binoculars or a telescope are a great advantage, but they are by no means essential. In fact, it is probably a good thing not to

buy binoculars when you first start, as the lack of them will encourage you to become more skilled at stalking birds.

Having got close enough to the birds, what do you look for? The answer is 'everything'. But your first priority is to identify them. **How to identify birds** on

9

page 12 is a suggested list of points to note.

Making notes

If you have not taken your field guide with you, it can be very difficult to remember all the necessary information until you get home. Also, you may see several 'new' birds on the same day. Therefore, when out birdwatching, always carry a notebook and pencil so that you can immediately record your sightings.

Before going on your first field trip it is a good idea to practise making notes on the common garden birds. Then you will be ready to make detailed notes on any rarity you may see. Remember, rough sketches, labelled with the distinguishing marks such as eye-stripe or wing-bars and the colours, are often far quicker than a long description. (See **How to sketch birds** on page 60.)

A permanent record

Your field records are only rough notes. It is useful to keep a permanent record as you never know when you will want to refer back. There are several ways you can write up your notes. You may prefer a loose-leaf file, a set of cards or a permanent record book. It depends on how you want to arrange your entries. You may want to keep a simple diary or have a series of species headings with notes on behaviour at different times of the year. Remember, whatever system you choose, your notes are made to be used, so make sure you can refer easily and quickly to any particular point. Your notebooks may never be read by anyone else, but they can be a great source of pleasure by bringing back memories of exciting days birdwatching in many different places.

Binoculars

As your birdwatching improves, you will want a pair of binoculars. One of the most important aspects to remember when buying a pair is size and weight. The magnification of binoculars is classified with two numbers, for example 8×20. Eight indicates the number of times the picture is enlarged, and 20 is the size of the object lens. The larger the lens, the bigger and heavier the binoculars.

An important point to bear in mind is that the more the bird is magnified, the more your own movements are magnified, and large binoculars are rather difficult to hold steady. A popular size of binoculars for the birdwatcher is 8×30. These are light to carry round your neck and good models can be bought fairly inexpensively. As to the manufacturer, this is very much a personal choice and it is always best to test a pair in the field before buying them.

The final stage

Having become an accomplished birdwatcher, you will have realised that part of the fun of birdwatching is knowing what birds to expect at certain times of the year. **A birdwatcher's calendar** on page 74 tells you which birds to expect each month.

As you travel round the country, perhaps on holiday, you will notice that different species of birds live in different areas. At the coast you may see a fulmar. This bird spends most of its life at sea, but comes onto the cliffs to breed. If you visit the West Country, Wales or Scotland, you may see a buzzard; this bird is seldom seen in the east of England. There are certain birds that live in Scotland, such as the crested tit and capercaillie, which do not occur in England, Ireland or Wales. Bird distribution is just one of the fascinating topics you will be able to study in depth.

Jay

E. A. Janes

How to Identify Birds

When trying to identify a 'new' bird, it is often very difficult to know what main points to look for, especially if it is only visible for a moment. Here is a suggested list of the points you should try to note while the bird is still in front of you.

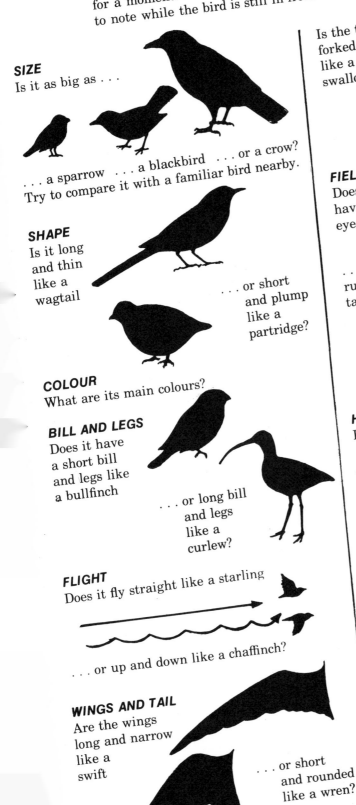

SIZE
Is it as big as . . .

. . . a sparrow . . . a blackbird . . . or a crow?
Try to compare it with a familiar bird nearby.

SHAPE
Is it long and thin like a wagtail

. . . or short and plump like a partridge?

COLOUR
What are its main colours?

BILL AND LEGS
Does it have a short bill and legs like a bullfinch

. . . or long bill and legs like a curlew?

FLIGHT
Does it fly straight like a starling

. . . or up and down like a chaffinch?

WINGS AND TAIL
Are the wings long and narrow like a swift

. . . or short and rounded like a wren?

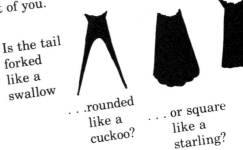

Is the tail forked like a swallow

. . .rounded like a cuckoo?

. . . or square like a starling?

FIELD MARKS
Does it have an eye-stripe

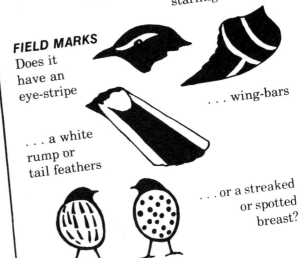

. . . wing-bars

. . . a white rump or tail feathers

. . . or a streaked or spotted breast?

HABITS
Does it climb trees like a woodpecker
. . . wag its tail like a wagtail
. . . feed on the ground like a dunnock
. . . or in the air like a swallow?

VOICE
What is its call or song?

WHERE IS IT FOUND?

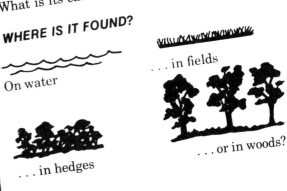

On water

. . . in fields

. . . in hedges

. . . or in woods?

WHEN IS IT FOUND?
All the year round . . .
only in summer like a swift . . .
. . . or only in winter like a brambling?

Bird for all Seasons

The ptarmigan lives on open, rocky mountainsides in western Europe, mainly at heights of 2000 to 10,000 feet above sea level. Few people see the bird except for a handful of mountaineers and, of course, birdwatchers.

The ptarmigan is a bird left behind by the ice age. It has always fascinated naturalists, because its colour changes with the seasons. It is the only species of its family to have three distinct plumages; in addition to those of summer and winter, there is a special autumn colouring. The ptarmigan is indeed a master of the art of camouflage, and each of its successive plumages blends superbly with its surroundings.

The ptarmigan belongs to the grouse family, Tetraonidae. It is slightly smaller than a pigeon but much heavier, weighing up to a pound or more. It measures 12 to 14 inches from bill to tail, and has most distinctive feet, which are feathered right to the claws, enabling the bird to walk on fresh snow without sinking in very far. In winter the foot is so thickly covered in fine feathers that it

looks like the paw of a hare; hence its scientific name Lagopus, the Latin for 'hare's foot'.

In the Alps, the ptarmigan lives all the year round at between 6000 and 10,000 feet. It takes a really bad snowstorm to drive the bird down from these bleak heights to the shelter of the nearest trees, and at the first opportunity it returns to its proper place on the rugged mountainside.

The bird moults three times a year. Like the mountain hare, it turns pure white in November — except for the tail, which stays black all the year round. (When a ptarmigan is resting, its tail is almost completely hidden by the white tail coverts.) The cock bird in winter also has a black band running from the base of the bill to just behind the eye. In spite of this dark mark, the bird's camouflage is so good that you need an eagle's eye to pick it out with field-glasses on the snowy slopes where it lives.

In mid-April, when the stoat and mountain hare are beginning to change into their summer coats, the ptarmigan grows dark brown or grey feathers, or — especially in

females — beige or yellow ones. This spring moult begins on the head and neck, spreads to the breast, flanks, and under the tail, and finally colours the back and parts of the wings.

However, the moult does not affect the rest of the body, so that when the bird is in full breeding plumage, at about the end of May, it is still half white. This patterning, half white, half brown, makes the ptarmigan difficult to see against its background of rock and snow. Like many other camouflaged animals, the ptarmigan 'freezes' when anyone approaches, pressing itself against the ground to hide the belly and flight feathers, which are still white. If you are out skiing at this time of year, you can get very close to a ptarmigan without knowing it is there — that is, until there is a sudden flash of white wings and a "belching" call.

In August and September the bird undergoes a complete moult, becoming much greyer for a short time. Then, with the coming of the first autumn moult, the dark feathers are gradually replaced. At about the end of October or middle of November most ptarmigans in

the Alps are, like the mountain hares, once again clad magnificently in white.

In winter, ptarmigans gather into flocks which can be quite a size. They spend the night under the snow, using their feet to make small holes or burrows where they are sheltered from the wind and harsh temperatures of the mountain. They never go to their sleeping quarters on foot, for this would leave a scent for foxes, which are their chief enemy at this time of year. Instead they fly to the lower slopes, drop on the snow, and excavate a hollow. Once hidden, they do not show themselves again until dawn.

An extraordinary sight greets a skier out in the early morning. Just as he is drinking in the utter peace and solitude of the mountains, little white balls break

Top: a ptarmigan in mid-April, soon after the beginning of the spring moult. By mid-May (above) this moult has spread from the head and neck to the breast, back and flanks. Both these birds are males, distinguished in winter by a black line from the bill to the eye, and in summer by being a darker brown than the female.

through the surface of the snow one by one, popping up in a landscape that had seemed totally deserted. Suddenly coming to life, the birds set off together for the windswept heights to find food.

Ptarmigans are very hardy birds. They are almost exclusively vegetarian. Before winter they cram their crops with every kind of vegetation they can find. This helps them survive periods of severe weather that no other bird could endure.

The ptarmigan is really an Arctic creature. Since the end of the last ice age the European 'snow grouse' has lived on as far south as the Alps, as if on an Arctic island in the temperate zone. This bird is beautifully adapted to its harsh environment, and to the comings and goings of the snow on the great mountains.

Top: two adult ptarmigans at the end of September, in autumn plumage. The male is on the right. The photograph (below right) taken in mid-October shows a female that has partially moulted into its winter plumage. Even at this intermediate stage the bird is well camouflaged, for the snow does not yet completely cover the ground. Bottom: the female's full winter plumage.

The upper and lower photographs on the left show both sexes in full breeding plumage. The female (lower left) is usually flecked with yellow, while the male (upper left) is darker. The above picture, taken in mid-September, shows a female in autumn plumage.

Many people who are interested in birds collect parts of dead specimens; this is not as nasty as it sounds! A bird's plumage is very beautiful; even individual feathers are very attractive and make a colourful, as well as useful, collection. I once found a sparrow-hawk's 'kill' and although the features of the victim were very distinctive, I could not think from which bird they had come. By taking the tail feathers home and comparing them with my own feather collection, I was able to prove that it had in fact come from a juvenile cuckoo.

Birds' wings are useful for people who paint and draw; they enable the artist to choose the exact colour and also get the wing structure correct. I find it useful to have a reference collection of wings, feathers and feet and often I find parts of birds which need identifying.

Wings

During the summer you will quite often find freshly killed birds by the roadside; very often these are young birds which are not quick enough to get out of the way of the passing cars. Adult birds are also killed in this way. During one year in Bedfordshire, I found a swallow, cuckoo, whitethroat, skylark and a red-legged part-ridge as well as starlings, black-birds and sparrows—all had been killed by cars. Many of these had only received slight injuries, sufficient to kill them, but other-wise leaving them in perfect con-dition. It was possible to take the wings off these birds and build up a collection.

The fresher the corpse the easier it is to take the wings off. Place the dead bird on its back and spread out one of the wings, feel along the bone at the top of the wing and cut it at the second joint (see illustration). With small birds this is easy, but difficulty may arise with larger ones. To sever the wing completely it is necessary to break the bone and cut the tendon. By cutting the second joint one loses some of the scapular feathers—the small wing feathers near the body, which in ducks is unfortunate as they may be very colourful. This leaves the minimum amount of muscle which is likely to smell. If there is some meat left on the bone, it is possible to prevent it from smelling by rubbing it with salt. However, out of my collection of over forty wings only one had too strong a smell to be kept indoors, and that was the wing of a mute swan!

After death the wing stiffens up. The length of time varies with the size of the bird, but generally small birds' wings set in about three or four days, while larger wings take longer; the evil smelling swan's wing took almost five weeks!

When building up a collection it is a good plan to take both wings from a dead bird and place one in the open position and the other closed. In this way you will have the wings in the most useful positions for drawing or painting. To set a wing open, I use card-board-box lids as setting boards (shoe-box lids are ideal) and push two pins through the muscle, then, holding the first primary, gently spread the wing into its flying position and push a third pin between the first and second primary (see illustration). One of the best methods of mounting a wing once it is set is to sew it with a single loop of cotton to a sheet of

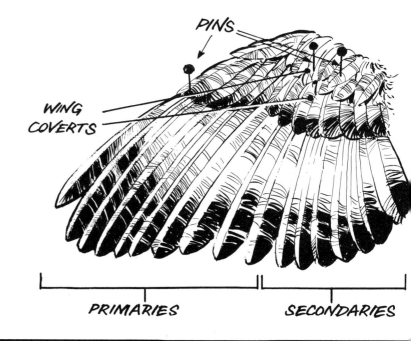

PINS

WING COVERTS

PRIMARIES

SECONDARIES

● *by Peter Holden*

card. When the wing is mounted it should be labelled with the bird's species, sex, date and place where it was found.

In order to prevent feather-lice or moths from damaging your collection, you should put naphthalene crystals or moth balls in the drawer or box where the collection is kept.

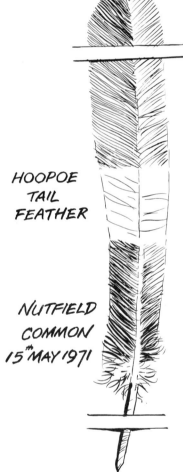

HOOPOE TAIL FEATHER

NUTFIELD COMMON 15ᵗʰ MAY 1971

Feathers

Although feathers are easier to find, they are more difficult to identify than wings. Therefore it is better to collect feathers from dead birds so that they can be correctly identified. If you find a corpse the best feathers to take are the primary wing and tail feathers.

A good source of supply is a wildfowl collection where you will probably find many. If you visit a zoo you may be able to obtain some feathers by asking one of the keepers.

One suggestion for mounting feathers is to take a blank sheet of cartridge paper and to fix it, at the edges only, to a piece of card the same size. The feather is then held on the paper and its position marked in pencil. Two pairs of horizontal lines are cut in the paper so that the top and bottom of the feather are held in place (see illustration). Do not use glue or Sellotape as this will damage the feathers.

As with wings, naphthalene crystals should be kept with the collection.

Feet

Feet, although making the least colourful collection, show many fascinating features characteristic of various groups of birds. The webbed feet of duck, the lobed toes of coot, two toes backwards and two forwards of the woodpecker and the powerful talons of the bird of prey.

The foot of a dead bird should be cut off above the tarsus joint— the first joint above the toe (see illustration). If the bird has died recently, it will be possible to move the toes and the foot can be mounted immediately. However, soon after a bird has died the foot becomes stiff. If this has happened leave the foot in cold water until it softens.

Then cut a piece of wire about half an inch longer than the leg

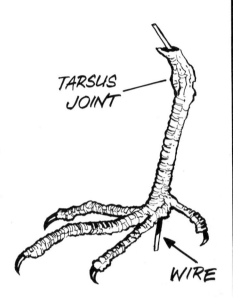

TARSUS JOINT

WIRE

portion that remains (vary the thickness of the wire according to the size of the foot). Push the wire down the back of the leg and out at the bottom of the foot, until it is flush with the tarsus joint and half an inch protrudes at the base. Bend the half-inch forward and push it through some stiff cardboard and fasten at the back with Sellotape.

Normally the toes will spread out naturally, but with webbed feet it is best to pin the toes apart so that the webbing lies flat. A coat of clear varnish preserves the foot as well as making it more attractive. As with other collections, label each foot fully.

● NOTE Always remember to wash your hands after touching a dead bird.

A warden's winter

Have you ever visited an RSPB reserve? If so, did you notice what the warden was doing? The chances are that he was in a reception hut ready to greet you and tell you what birds had been seen that day. Meeting visitors and keeping an eye open for unusual birds on the reserve are important aspects of a warden's work, but, as the photographs on these pages show, he has many

other jobs to do, particularly in winter, when there are no breeding birds to be disturbed and unwanted vegetation is easier to remove.

Many of the winter tasks involve reserve management; this means the warden looks after the reserve so that it is a suitable place for birds to live in. Often special requirements have to be provided for rare species, which means that certain areas on some reserves are maintained artificially; expanses of open water are defended against gradual invasion by reeds, pebble islands are kept clear of colonising vegetation.

Leighton Moss lies between the Lancashire coast and the hills of the Lake District. It is a wet valley which if left to itself would first of all be covered by reeds and later be taken over by alder and willow trees. The warden, John Wilson and his assistant, David Mower keep the reeds in check by cutting and spraying, and then use some of them to build screens that conceal visitors as they approach the hides. They also replace some of the willows on the drier ground with alder, buckthorn, guelder rose, and other species to attract a greater variety of birds.

While the main purpose of a

bird reserve is to conserve birds and their habitats, wherever possible the public is given an opportunity of watching them. This means putting up hides and encouraging the birds to come into view. Dead trees and logs are positioned by open water to provide perching places, and at Leighton Moss floating islands of iris are staked down in front of the hide; one island has attracted 800 snipe.

The public causeway and

3. Paths are built up using waste from a quarry. 4. A path of railway sleepers, out of reach of winter floods. 5. Cutting and laying reeds for a screen. 6. A daily log is kept of birds seen on the reserve.

other paths through the reserve have suffered heavy winter flooding and to overcome this problem the wardens shovelled some 2000 tons of quarry waste into trailers and spread it on the paths. The public causeway is now always clear of water, and has several permanent nature trail signs.

As if all this is not enough, there are daily weather readings to take, a moth trap to operate, a daily log and regular reports to write on birds and management for RSPB headquarters, enquiries from the public on a wide range of topics, and lectures to give to local societies.

Do-it-yourself: NESTBOX

Here is an inexpensive do-it-yourself nestbox which will attract hole-nesting birds such as blue tits, great tits, tree sparrows and nuthatches.

Materials required

A 6"×¼" unplaned board approximately 4' 9" long; two dozen 1½" nails; a few tacks and a 6"×2" strip of rubber, waterproof canvas or leather. Buy softwood; cedar is probably best as it lasts well, but ordinary deal or pine is cheaper and can be treated to prevent rot; hardwood is more difficult to work and is expensive.

Construction

Cut the board in lengths as shown in fig. 2. The exact length of the back does not matter as the projections top and bottom are simply used for attaching to the tree or post.

If you tilt the saw sideways slightly when making the cut between the front and the roof (cut XX), you will neatly provide yourself with a sloping top edge for the front and a sloping back edge for the roof; this angled cut should be made so that the front of the front is about ¼" less than the 8".

The hole in the front should be 1⅛" in diameter, with its top 1" down from the top of the front; a 10p piece is the correct size. Cutting the hole is far easier than you might imagine; if you do not own an electric drill or a hand-brace and bit, you can use a coping saw.

Nail the box together in this order: one side to the back, then the base, the other side and last of all the front. Before nailing the front, lay the roof in position to make sure that the front does not project too high. (See figs. 1 and 3.)

For a hinge use a 6"×2" strip of thick rubber (old car inner tube is ideal), waterproof canvas or leather, nailed to the back and roof. Although this will need renewing occasionally, it will not rust and provides a waterproof join at the back of the box.

It is advisable to hook the roof down at both sides with clips. Alternatively, it can be nailed or screwed down; this has the advantage that you will not be tempted to open it too frequently and disturb the occupants.

If you treat the box with preservative, on the outside only, it will last longer.

The box should be placed between 4 and 16 feet high in trees, bushes or buildings. It should not be positioned in direct sunlight or into a prevailing wind.

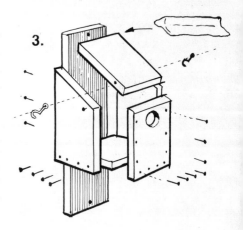

2.	8"	10"		X			
6" Side		Side	Front	Roof	Base	Back	6"
10"		8"	8"	X 8½"	4½"	18"	

● by John Taunton

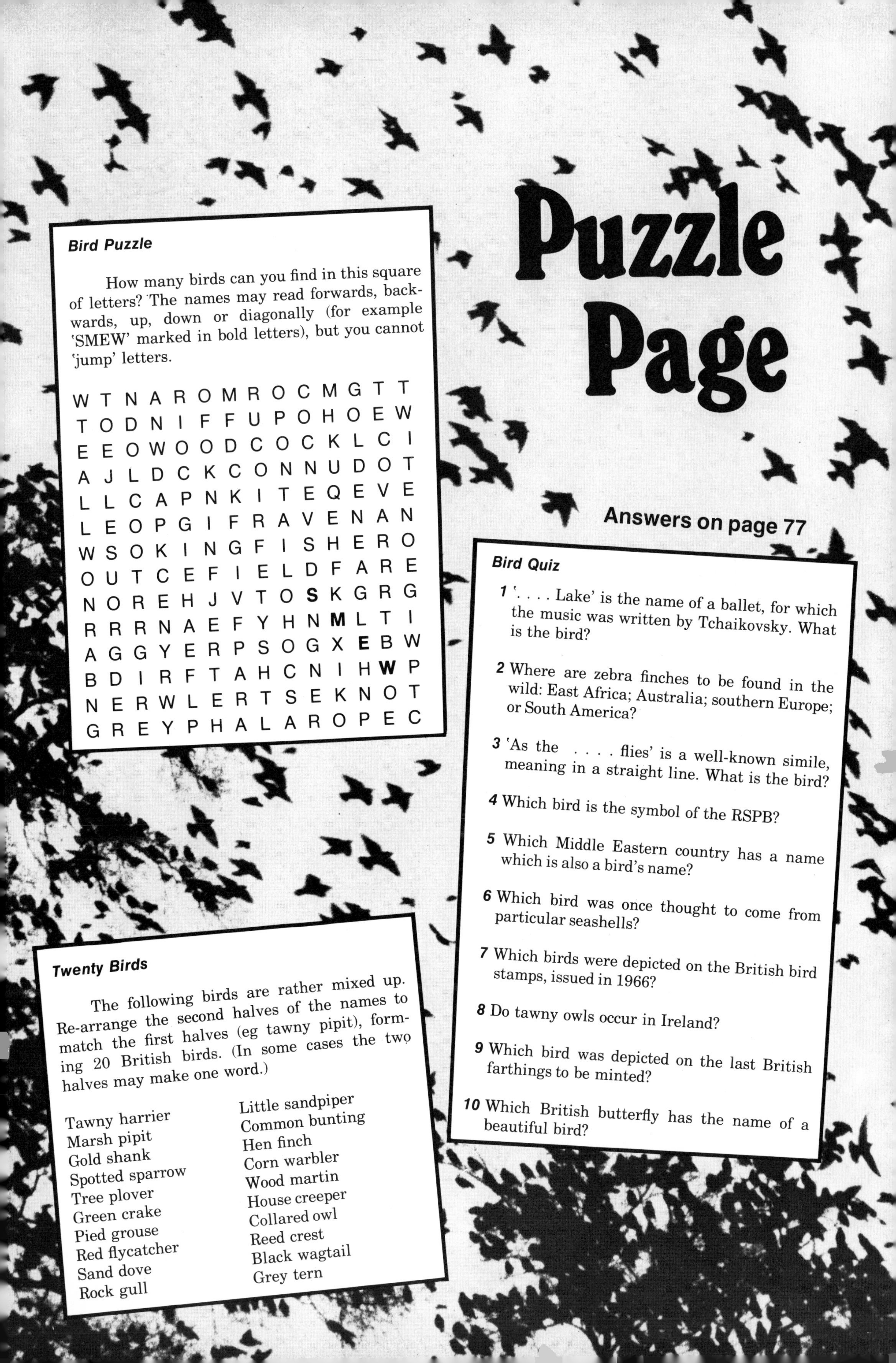

Puzzle Page

Answers on page 77

Bird Puzzle

How many birds can you find in this square of letters? The names may read forwards, backwards, up, down or diagonally (for example 'SMEW' marked in bold letters), but you cannot 'jump' letters.

```
W T N A R O M R O C M G T T
T O D N I F F U P O H O E W
E E O W O O D C O C K L C I
A J L D C K C O N N U D O T
L L C A P N K I T E Q E V E
L E O P G I F R A V E N A N
W S O K I N G F I S H E R O
O U T C E F I E L D F A R E
N O R E H J V T O S K G R G
R R R N A E F Y H N M L T I
A G G Y E R P S O G X E B W
B D I R F T A H C N I H W P
N E R W L E R T S E K N O T
G R E Y P H A L A R O P E C
```

Bird Quiz

1 '. . . . Lake' is the name of a ballet, for which the music was written by Tchaikovsky. What is the bird?

2 Where are zebra finches to be found in the wild: East Africa; Australia; southern Europe; or South America?

3 'As the . . . . flies' is a well-known simile, meaning in a straight line. What is the bird?

4 Which bird is the symbol of the RSPB?

5 Which Middle Eastern country has a name which is also a bird's name?

6 Which bird was once thought to come from particular seashells?

7 Which birds were depicted on the British bird stamps, issued in 1966?

8 Do tawny owls occur in Ireland?

9 Which bird was depicted on the last British farthings to be minted?

10 Which British butterfly has the name of a beautiful bird?

Twenty Birds

The following birds are rather mixed up. Re-arrange the second halves of the names to match the first halves (eg tawny pipit), forming 20 British birds. (In some cases the two halves may make one word.)

Tawny harrier
Marsh pipit
Gold shank
Spotted sparrow
Tree plover
Green crake
Pied grouse
Red flycatcher
Sand dove
Rock gull

Little sandpiper
Common bunting
Hen finch
Corn warbler
Wood martin
House creeper
Collared owl
Reed crest
Black wagtail
Grey tern

Make your garden

House sparrow

a bird reserve

Three feet from my head the window-pane is rattling. Not because it is windy, but because three blue tits are hammering away at the peanuts inside a wire basket attached to the glass by a rubber sucker. If I stop work and look out of the window (and I do that far too often), I can see a willow tit feeding on the bird table. Underneath two dunnocks are foraging about for seeds. There is a robin, a chaffinch and a blackbird on the lawn, and a pair of grey wagtails nesting in a hole in the dry stone wall. Now you may say that I am lucky to live in the country and near the sea, and that we can't all have willow tits and grey wagtails outside our windows, but the fact is that you can get the most astonishing variety of birds to come and live wherever you want them to, providing you supply the right living conditions and the right food. Even a window-sill can attract birds if you fix a bird-table to it. But of course it is not interesting to a bird until you start putting out the food!

The great thing is to try and imagine that you are a bird and work out what sort of conditions you are looking for. The results may surprise you. Take, for example, the common pigeon you see in towns. All these 'feral' pigeons are descended from the rock dove, a bird that lives in the wild conditions of the sea coast and cliffs, foraging along the cliff-tops and rough pastureland for its food. You might think that a street pigeon lives a very different life. But not at all. The sheer height of the buildings in a city centre are its cliffs. The crevices and ledges of an ornate town hall or public library are the cliff ledges, where it will build its nest. Perhaps it even be-

Swallows

lieves the roar of traffic down below sounds like the sea! When it needs food, the pigeon will forage in the pastures of the parks and gardens, although of course it has learnt to look for scraps of food that soft-hearted man supplies.

Food

Here's what to bear in mind; sooner or later birds will learn to use your nesting-sites and take your food, but you can help them along by providing the facilities in an intelligent manner. If your house has a hedge of some kind to mark a boundary, don't let anyone cut it down. Many birds like to

shelter or nest in a hedge of hawthorn or holly. If you haven't got a hedge then plant one. Try not to let people make the garden too tidy. An overgrown area of bushes or brambles is something to preserve carefully, although of course you may have to keep it in bounds. Variety is perhaps the key to attracting birds—different levels of garden, different shrubs and plants, corners, stone walls with plenty of crevices and cracks. Wrens love to scout around a wall and search for bugs and insects of all kinds.

Remember that you can roughly divide birds into two groups, seed-eaters and live-food

● *by Tony Soper*

eaters. For the seed-eaters you may like to leave one weedy patch in your garden. Gardeners may not love thistles but goldfinches certainly do. If you can't persuade gardeners to leave a stinging-nettle patch, then try suggesting

sunflowers. Point out that the craze for tidiness is a very unnatural one, and suggest a bit of 'planned disorder'. One of the reasons for the current national water-shortage is that well-meaning but ignorant authorities drain marshes and boggy places, reclaiming them for grazing. This makes it all too easy for rain-water to rush straight off to the sea instead of filling up the marsh 'sponge', and draining slowly in time of drought.

Water

Water is most important for birds, just as it is for us. In fact none of them can manage without it. They get a certain amount from the food they eat, but they obtain the rest by drinking. Tree-living species may sip from the foliage after the rain, but most birds will visit ponds and streams. They also need water to keep their plumage in order. Feathers have to be kept in good condition, and birds must bathe before they can start to preen properly. Incidentally some birds actually bathe in flight; swallows and swifts dive down to the water's surface and take a quick dip as they flash by. And again, some birds bathe in dust, but that's another story.

So you will see, if you are hoping to attract birds it's most important to provide water. The easiest way is just to put down a bowl of water, but there are a number of problems you should bear in mind. The water should be shallow, an inch or two is quite enough. Make sure the bowl or dish isn't too slippery so that the birds can get a good grip. An upturned dustbin lid makes a very good bird bath. Remember that cats like birds too, so don't put the water too close to a place where cats might lurk. Birds get very excited about their bathing and they may forget to keep a proper watch.

Of course the best bath of all is a proper pond with varying levels of water and with fresh-water plants. Quite apart from its usefulness to birds, this will also provide living space for lots of amphibious creatures like frogs, toads and newts, and a natural home for many other interesting pond animals. If you have it stocked with sticklebacks and goldfish you may be visited by a heron one day, although the fish won't welcome him as much as you will.

Nestboxes

When you've made your garden attractive to birds—full of nesting-sites and food plants, you may want to go further and increase the bird population in your garden still more. Now you will have to use artificial nestboxes and supply special food on bird tables and ground trays. You can buy excellent nestboxes from the RSPB of course, but in many ways it's more fun and certainly more satisfying to make your own. This is one of the occasions when you don't have to be an expert as a carpenter because the birds won't mind if your corners aren't square and if your roof is all a bit askew! The instructions for building a nestbox are on page 20.

Put your nestboxes in posi-

tions where they don't get the full force of the sun, and where they are in reasonable cover. But make sure they aren't in a position where cats can get at them. The height you attach them isn't very important, but obviously they will want to be off the ground and out of the way of interference. It's awfully difficult to stop yourself going to examine the box every few minutes to see if it's occupied, but this is the one certain way of making sure that the birds won't have anything to do with it.

Bird tables

Bird tables are the obvious way of giving extra food; do put some food on the ground as well for those species, like blackbirds and dunnocks, which prefer to stay at ground level. Again you can buy a bird table but you may prefer to knock up your own. Details are given on page 41.

You want to put a variety of food on your bird table and it's quite surprising what some birds will eat. Almost any kind of cheese is a success, but the food that seems to be most successful is the peanut. Our birds eat over three pounds of peanuts every week! Again, though, you must remember the seed-eaters. You can go out collecting wild-flower seeds in the autumn, or of course you can buy seeds in the shops; the cheapest way is to buy in bulk. The difficulty about feeding seeds is that if you just put them on the bird table they get blown about all over the place and wasted. So you have to put them in a seed hopper which also keeps the grain dry.

Even if you only throw a few crusts on the lawn your birds will be glad of it, especially in the winter months, but of course the more kinds of food you offer, and the more varied ways you present it, will influence the species and the numbers you attract. But whatever you do, please remember that if you start feeding birds you must not stop suddenly. In a hard winter many birds will soon learn to rely on you for food; it is important not to let them down. Start making your bird garden now. I wish you luck with it.

Blackbird

G. St. J. Hollis

David and Katie Urry

Puffin

Ard

For six years now I have been going to the most westerly point of the United Kingdom mainland, 20 miles further west than Land's End, for my holidays. The beautiful scenery made by extinct volcanoes, the wildlife and the delightful weather make us return to western Ardnamurchan. From the ruin of one of the unique volcanoes, especially at sunset, the Outer Hebridean islands of Eigg, Muck, Canna and Rhum show themselves on the horizon.

When we go fishing in our small dingy, we watch many birds which we would never even see from the mainland. For example, one day when out in the boat we saw hundreds of different birds all

Common Seal pup

Oystercatcher *Stephen Dalton (N.H.P.A.)*

Razorbi

namurchan Holidays

Gannet

Werner Curth (Ardea)

Red-throated diver

Bobby Tulloch (Bruce Coleman)

Shag

in one small area. There must have been at least 50 gannets all diving into the water. The water around was covered with other seabirds: puffins, razorbills, cormorants, shags, common and black guillemots, terns, shearwaters and, of course, the gulls. We think the cause of this gathering was a large shoal of small fish which were being chased by a shoal of larger fish. The birds, perhaps because of the abundance of food, were unperturbed by our presence and we studied them at leisure.

Another time, when we were out in the boat, we saw a black bird chasing terns and gulls. From its tail we identified it as an arctic skua. The chasing did not stop until the victim dropped its fish, or regurgitated its last meal in order to flee more rapidly from the skua.

One day, when returning from our lobster pots with a fine, blue lobster in the bottom of the boat, we saw four birds flying overhead. When they landed on the water we easily identified them by the grey head with white streaks down the back of the neck and the blaze of red at the throat; they were red-throated divers.

When out walking we have seen a golden eagle, and many buzzards which are quite common on Ardnamurchan. Another bird of prey inhabiting these parts is the peregrine falcon. Peregrines are easily distinguished by their distinctive flight; rapid flapping alternating with long glides.

For the all-round naturalist, we have seen otters, deer and seals; although we have not seen any, wild cats are known to frequent the area. Orchids grow in profusion, especially near the peat bogs; felworts and other gentians, tutsan and gráss of Parnassus can be found if one looks hard enough.

Over the years we have ticked off more than 50 species of birds but many more inhabit Ardnamurchan. Although the weather is not always good, the beautiful scenery, unique geological volcanic formations and wildlife always make the holiday well worthwhile.

Unfortunately, our last holiday ended on a sad note; one of the red-throated divers was washed up dead on the shore. It was not till we saw the bird close to that we realised its infinite beauty.

 by Nigel Wilkinson YOC member

Beachcombing for birds

Have you ever shuffled along the tide-line to see what has been brought in? Driftwood, bottles, car tyres, plastic buoys; the list is endless. But the RSPB is interested in one particular find – birds.

Bodies of dead or sick birds are often washed up by the tide. The number of bodies found is a rough indication of how many birds are dying at sea. So if, for example, there is an oil spill from a ship at sea, the seriousness of the spill can be estimated from the number of birds washed ashore.

The RSPB runs a Beached Bird Survey in which it asks people to regularly count the dead birds they find on beaches. On five week-ends each winter, about 500 people throughout Britain and Ireland, including many YOC groups, cover more than 1000 miles of beaches, looking for dead birds.

During the five surveys in the winter of 1973-74 nearly 4900 birds were found and a quarter of them were oiled. In February an international survey is held, and beaches in Denmark, Holland, Germany, Belgium and France are patrolled in the same way, and results compared.

Gulls are the commonest birds that are found, but guillemots and other members of the auk family are the most frequent victims of oil spills. Sometimes rare birds are washed up, such as the white-billed diver which was picked up in the Firth of Clyde in 1973, or the Brünnich's guillemots which have turned up on the Cumbrian coast. So it is always worth taking a close look at the corpses you discover. You never know, you might find a rarity.

Sometimes sick or oiled birds can be rescued alive on the beach. Although they are pathetic and helpless, these birds have little chance of survival. Often they have swallowed oil whilst trying to preen it off the feathers, and this can poison them. If you do find a sick bird, you must keep it warm and in the dark – a cardboard box is best – and hand it over as soon as possible to someone like an RSPCA inspector who is

experienced in cleaning and looking after birds.

Many birds die as a result of oil spilled at sea; in 1973 nearly a thousand died in spills off the coast of Ayrshire, while the historical oil spill from the oil-tanker *Torrey Canyon* off Land's End in 1967 killed at least 10,000 birds. We need to regularly search beaches for oiled birds so we can show the oil companies just how many birds are being killed through their carelessness. Then perhaps they will take steps to reduce oil spillages. If you live near the sea and feel you would like to take part in the Beached Bird Survey, please contact your YOC group leader if you are a member of the YOC or write to the research department at The Lodge, Sandy, Bedfordshire, SG19 2DL.

● *by Clare Lloyd*

Flightless birds

The flightless birds which live today have all evolved from flying ancestors. These, in their turn, evolved from small, lizard-like animals called pseudosuchians which lived some 200 million years ago.

Most flightless birds are found on islands where they have been isolated and where there are no predators to prevent a ground-living species from flourishing. They have no need of flight as a means of escape, nor for seeking food, as there is ample on the ground or in the sea.

In these circumstances, various groups have developed specialised abilities. The marine habitat of the penguin has led to the modification of the wings for highly efficient underwater propulsion. They have become flattened, stiff but flexible flippers. A sleeping penguin will still tuck its bill under its 'wing' — a reminder of its flying forefathers.

The flightless cormorant of the Galapagos retains the family habit of holding out its wings to dry, although these are now stubby and useless for flight.

Such island species were tame and therefore very vulnerable to the sudden arrival of ruthless predators in the form of mariners, hungry for fresh food. The sailors brought their dogs and cats, pigs and rats. A number of bird species, unable to survive, became extinct as a direct result of man's greed and thoughtlessness. It was the lighthouse-keeper's cat that totally wiped out the flightless St Stephen's Island wren. The whole population was exterminated within months of its discovery in 1894. The dodo, the solitaire — a close relative of the dodo — and the great auk are further classic examples.

Many flightless birds developed in New Zealand, the home of the extinct moas, which were large, flightless birds, ranging from the size of a turkey to giants standing 13 feet tall. Present-day species include the takahe and the weka, both members of the rail family, the same family as the moorhen and coot. The large weka, or New Zealand wood rail, has turned the tables on introduced rats and mice and added them to its own diet. The kakapo, or owl parrot, is wholly nocturnal; a ground runner and tree climber, it uses its wings for support and balance. At night it scampers down the hillsides with great agility to its grassland feeding grounds.

Perhaps the best known flightless species is New Zealand's own national bird — the strange, nocturnal kiwi. The kiwi is a member of the group of flightless birds known as 'ratities' which includes the ostrich, cassowary and rhea. Their loss of flight occurred many millions of years ago, but they still have very small, vestigial wings. Most grew to a great size, developing powerful legs for running and a terrestrial mode of life, occupying much the same niche as the grazing mammals. In Africa it is quite usual to see ostriches among the herds of zebra and antelope on the plains.

Humboldt penguin

● *by Robert Gillmor*

31

Sunday – March 24

Early in March, the *RSPB* had received a confidential letter informing me that a Mr X was to visit Scotland in search of golden eagle eggs. We took the matter very seriously and soon discovered that, accompanied by a friend, he would be travelling on the overnight train from Euston, arriving at Inverness on Sunday 24 March. It was my job to follow them. On Wednesday 20 March I drove to Edinburgh for talks with George Waterston, assistant director of the *RSPB* for Scotland, and we went carefully over the *ordnance survey* maps, discussing the likely areas that our 'suspects' would tackle. I was also given a list of gamekeepers of north Scotland whose keen eyes and help I would almost certainly need.

SUNDAY 24TH MARCH.

WHEN'S THE LONDON TRAIN DUE?

IT WILL BE IN ANY MINUTE NOW SIR.

THE LONDON TRAIN ARRIVES.

THAT COULD BE THE ONE.

PORTER

RICHARD PORTER TAKES A DISCREET LOOK AT THE TRAVELLING COMPANION OF MR X.

FOUR BAGS OF BULLS EYES PLEASE.

STOCKING UP FOR A JOURNEY SIR?

RICHARD PORTER TALKS TO THE PLAIN CLOTHES POLICEMAN SENT TO HELP.

O.K. I'LL LEAVE IT WITH YOU TO FOLLOW UP, BUT KEEP IN TOUCH YOU MAY NEED US.

THAT'S OUR MAN.

MR. X AND COMPANION LOAD THEIR GEAR INTO A WHITE VAUXHALL VICTOR.

NOW TO SEE IF WE ARE RIGHT THEY SEEM TO HAVE LOADS OF GEAR.

I THINK WE'LL HEAD NORTH TO START WITH.

32

RICHARD PORTER FOLLOWS THE VAUXHALL AT A SAFE DISTANCE...

I MUSTN'T GET TOO CLOSE – DON'T WANT THEM TO GET SUSPICIOUS AT THIS STAGE.

PYE 357F

RICHARD PORTER DECIDED TO CONTINUE NORTH AND WARN THE GAMEKEEPERS IN THAT AREA. HE VISITED THREE THE FOLLOWING DAY, THEN SPENT TWO MORE DAYS TOURING LOCHS ERIBOLL, HOPE, AND LOYAL PASSING ON INFORMATION.

THREE DAYS LATER OUTSIDE THE *ALTNAHARRA* HOTEL...

I'M TRYING TO CATCH UP WITH TWO FRIENDS OF MINE, SEEN ANYONE AROUND.

YES WE HAD A COUPLE OF GENTLEMEN HERE LAST NIGHT, THEY LEFT AN HOUR AGO.

RICHARD PORTER TALKS TO THE OWNER OF THE *CRASK INN*...

DO YOU KNOW WHEN THE OWNERS OF THE WHITE CAR ARE RETURNING.

WELL I DID SEE THEM HEADING INTO THE HILLS, BUT I DON'T KNOW WHY IN THIS WEATHER.

THE TWO COLLECTORS SET ABOUT THEIR THOUGHTLESS TASK IN APPALLING WEATHER CONDITIONS...

I CAN SEE THE NEST NOW, I THINK THE BIRD IS GOING TO LEAVE IT...

I CONTINUED SOUTH TOWARDS ARDGAY WHERE I HAD ARRANGED AN EVENING MEETING WITH GEORGE WATERSTON. IT WAS A DEPRESSING DAY – COLD WITH DRIVING RAIN – AND MY SPIRITS WERE SINKING. THE MOORS ON EITHER SIDE OF ME DISAPPEARED INTO THE MIST HOLDING THE SECRETS OF THEIR RARE NESTING BIRDS. SUDDENLY, THERE IT WAS – 'PYE' THE WHITE VAUXHALL VICTOR. I PULLED INTO THE SIDE OF THE ROAD BEHIND THE 'CRASK INN' THE ONLY BUILDING ON THIS DESOLATE MOOR, AND PROCEEDED TO WATCH...

THE WHITE VAUXHALL, MY LUCK'S IN.

AFTER SEVERAL HOURS TWO FIGURES TRAMP OUT OF THE MURK...

FROM THE COVER OF A STONE WALL RICHARD PORTER WATCHES THE TWO COLLECTORS...

A FINE CLUTCH OF EGGS

YES INDEED WELL WORTH GETTING WET FOR.

RICHARD PORTER CONTACTS GEORGE WATERSTON ASKING HIM TO MEET HIM...

I'VE FOUND THEM AGAIN GEORGE AND THEY BOOKED INTO THE *ALTGUISH HOTEL* TOMORROW NIGHT, SO I'LL MEET YOU ON THE ROAD SOUTH AND WE MAY BE ABLE TO GRAB THEM TODAY...

THE TWO COLLECTORS HEADED SOUTH, BUT TURNED OFF EAST TOWARDS THE COAST AND GOLSPIE. HOWEVER RICHARD WAS PRESENTED WITH A SMALL DILEMMA. HE HAD ALMOST RUN OUT OF PETROL, SO HAD TO BREAK OFF THE CHASE AND WAIT FOR GEORGE WATERSTON. AFTER MEETING UP, THE TWO MEN CARRIED ON THE CHASE, BUT AFTER A THOROUGH SEARCH OF THE GOLSPIE AREA THE WHITE VAUXHALL WAS NOT TO BE FOUND...

ITS NO GOOD GEORGE WE HAVE LOST THEM AGAIN, I THINK WE'LL CALL IT A DAY AND MEET AGAIN TOMORROW.

THE NEXT DAY, RICHARD TOURS SOME KNOWN EYRIES BUT THE TWO 'SUSPECTS' WERE NOT TO BE SEEN ANYWHERE...

THAT'S THE FOURTH EYRIE AND NOT A SIGN OF THEM.

OUR BEST BET'S THE *ALTGUISH HOTEL* TONIGHT WE *KNOW* THEY WILL BE THERE.

23.00 HOURS OUTSIDE THE *ALTGUISH HOTEL* THE DINGWALL POLICE ARRIVE, A FEW MINUTES LATER MR X AND HIS COMPANION DRIVE UP IN THE WHITE VAUXHALL...

O.K. CHAPS THIS LOOKS LIKE THEM.

I CHARGE YOU WITH THE ILLEGAL POSSESSION OF GOLDEN EAGLE'S EGGS WHICH HAVE BEEN TAKEN FROM EYRIES IN SCOTLAND DURING THE LAST FEW DAYS.

IN MAY, THE TWO MEN WERE FOUND GUILTY OF BEING IN POSSESSION OF RECENTLY TAKEN EGGS OF GOLDEN EAGLES, AND WERE EACH FINED £100. ON THE MAPS THAT WERE CONFISCATED FROM THE BOOT OF THEIR CAR WERE MARKED THE SITES OF OVER 70 GOLDEN EAGLE EYRIES, AND ALSO THE NESTS OF OTHER RARE SPECIES IN SCOTLAND. WE FELT OUR MISSION HAD BEEN WORTHWHILE...

37

BLA–C'

SNOWY OWL

Snowy owls always capture the imagination of birdwatchers. The very name conjures up a picture of a ghostly white bird in the desolate Arctic waste—and that picture is largely a true one.

One of the largest owls, the snowy owl must also be one of the loneliest. On the bleak and barren tundras of northern Canada, Greenland, Scandinavia and Siberia they hunt singly in the near darkness, gliding on powerful

yet silent wings, their keen golden yellow eyes quick to spot the slightest movement from a small animal or bird. Once seen, there is little chance of escape; a quick swoop and a flash of talons as powerful as an eagle's, and another meal is secured. During the daytime they generally sit huddled in the lee of a rock, avoiding the company of even their own kind.

In the Arctic, although some snowy owls have been known to

● by Bobby Tulloch

take animals as large as Arctic hares, and birds the size of eider ducks, their main food is lemmings, a vole-like rodent. These animals have an unusual life history of 'regular ups and downs' in numbers. The population builds up for several years to a point of over-abundance; this is then followed by 'crash' or large reduction, and mass starvation. For several years after the lemming will be very scarce. This cycle of events affects other creatures—such as the snowy owl—which preys on the lemmings. But in the almost total darkness of the Arctic winter, even when lemmings are plentiful, the owls cannot get at them, because they live in burrows deep under the snow. Now the owls must move south and look for other food.

Following good lemming years and the subsequent rearing of large families, snowy owls have sometimes wandered as far south as Britain, usually to the northern islands and mountains. These are normally young birds up to three or four years old which are not old enough to breed. The parents will not allow them to remain in the area where they were brought up as they would compete for food. In some territories, one of the first spring 'chores' of the male snowy owl is to clear all previous young (and other snowy owls) off his breeding ground.

In 1963, after a lapse of some years, there were reports of snowy owls having been seen in some parts of Shetland. I had the thrill of seeing my first ever on the hillside not far from my home in Yell. Little did I realise that a year or two later I would find a snowy owl's nest on Shetland—adding a new species to the British breeding list! One or two male snowy owls seemed to stay in Shetland between 1963 and 1966, but one day in January 1966 I came across a magnificent female bird on Fetlar. Even larger than the male, with plumage barred and spotted with brown, this was probably the same bird that nested on Fetlar the following year.

On 3 June 1967 I had taken a party of Swiss birdwatchers over to Fetlar. We were walking over the hill when a male snowy owl appeared on a rock not far away. By this time I had often seen snowy owls, but this bird had a glowering, almost menacing attitude which puzzled me! I left the party happily watching and took a walk round the back of the rocky outcrop. With mounting excitement I saw that a female owl had appeared from somewhere and was sitting watching me intently from a rock. Suddenly, almost at my feet, was a nest with three round white eggs! Without even stopping I walked past, and within the few minutes it took to rejoin the party I had decided that I could not take the risk of telling anyone about this terrific find. With great effort, I hid my excitement and without saying a word manoeuvred the people away to look for something else!

The nest was less than a mile from the nearest houses and, as the area was grazed by sheep and ponies and visited by the crofters, it seemed inevitable that the news of this event would soon leak out. The nest would then become a target, not only for birdwatchers with the best intentions, but possibly for egg-collectors. So it was decided that the RSPB would set up a round-the-clock watch from a safe vantage point, which would also serve as an observation post where interested people could get a glimpse of the owls.

During the month which followed, the female owl never left the nest for more than a few minutes each day. The male stayed on watch all day and went off at dusk to catch a rabbit, which he would present to his mate on the nest. It is doubtful whether the parent birds were as delighted as the wardens when, from the seven eggs laid, six young snowy owls were hatched!

The youngsters grew rapidly and after about two weeks began to leave the nest and hide in the rocks nearby; here their coats of mottled-grey down made them extremely difficult to spot. By the time they were six weeks old they could be seen making their first, unsteady attempts at flying.

Several hundred visitors made the trip to Fetlar to see the owls, and while disturbance from them was minimal there were a few anxious moments. Sheep and ponies grazed nearby and sometimes seemed to be dangerously close to the nest and had to be chased off by the wardens. Wandering parties of hooded crows often mobbed and harried the owls, and stole food from the young.

Many people thought it was unlikely that the owls would nest again, but, to our delight, they have returned each year to nest in almost exactly the same spot. Although they have never matched that great first effort, when six young were reared, they have never failed to bring up a family. So far, no other breeding pairs have been discovered in Shetland, but there are several remote and little-visited areas, and when all these young Fetlar birds have grown up—well, who knows?

After the discovery of the first snowy owl's nest, the RSPB applied to the Secretary of State for the area surrounding the nest to be declared a sanctuary, and permission was granted. In addition, it was arranged, with the permission of the owner and tenants of the land, for an area of about 1600 acres to be designated as the RSPB Fetlar reserve.

Apart from the snowy owls, this reserve contains many interesting and rare breeding birds, such as whimbrel, red-necked phalarope and great and Arctic skuas. Part of the reserve boundary is sea-coast, where, as well as large numbers of sea-birds, both grey and common seals breed, and otters are sometimes seen.

There can be little doubt that had it not been for the protection given by the RSPB the Fetlar snowy owls would never have nested successfully. From the two or three thousand signatures in the visitors' book, it goes to show that protection can be given without depriving anyone of the chance of watching one of the rarest and most magnificent of all our breeding birds.

Do-it-yourself:
BIRD TABLE

A well-stocked bird table is probably the surest way of attracting birds to your garden. All you need is a flat platform supported on a post or hung from a tree. Here are directions for a simple, do-it-yourself table costing very little.

Materials required

A 12″×18″ piece of exterior quality plywood, $\frac{1}{2}$″ thick; a 4′ 4″ length of 1″×1″ (approx.) wood; a dozen $1\frac{1}{4}$″ screws or nails; a means of supporting or hanging the bird table.

Note: It is important that the plywood is of **exterior** (or marine) quality, otherwise it will quickly split with rain or snow.

Construction

In order to prevent food from being blown off the table and yet to allow water to drain away, cut the 1″×1″ wood into two 12″ lengths and two 14″ lengths, and fix these along the top edges of the plywood, leaving a gap of about 1″ at each corner. Screw or nail right through the plywood from below; this will also help to prevent the ply from splitting at the edges. If you treat the wood with preservative such as **Cuprinol**, it will last longer.

Erecting

Your bird table can either be supported on a post or hung. It is simpler to hang it provided that you have a suitable tree.

Hanging type. Screw small screweyes into the wooden strips at each corner of the bird table. To each of these attach equal lengths (about 2 feet) of Terylene cord; a more expensive alternative is brass or galvanized chain. Tie the cords to a bough; to prevent the table from rotating in the wind, tie the cords in pairs, rather than to one central point.

1.

Post type. A wooden post, 2″×2″ is ideal — 5 feet high with an extra foot or so to drive into the ground.

Having driven in the post, the difficult part is attaching the table to it. If it is to be in a very sheltered place, a big screw and wide washer through the top of the table into the post might suffice; but a strong wind would soon lift this out and damage the table. Instead, you can screw four metal angle brackets to the table and post (see fig. 2); or better still, you can form a square recess under the table to take the post, using short lengths of 2″×1″ wood screwed through the table from the top and screwed to each other, fixing these to the post with a screw at each side (see fig. 3).

Extras

One or two hooks screwed into the side of the bird table are very useful for hanging chop bones, strings of peanuts or a food basket.

Finally, if you do not want to make a bird table, you can always buy one ready-made from the RSPB.

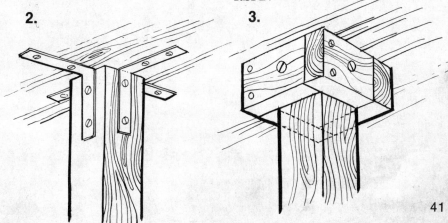

2.

3.

● *by John Taunton*

These eight pictures are photographs of birds, or parts of birds, and have been taken at rather unusual angles. From the parts you can see, you should be able to identify the birds.

Picture Quiz

Answers on page 77

6

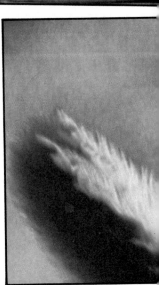

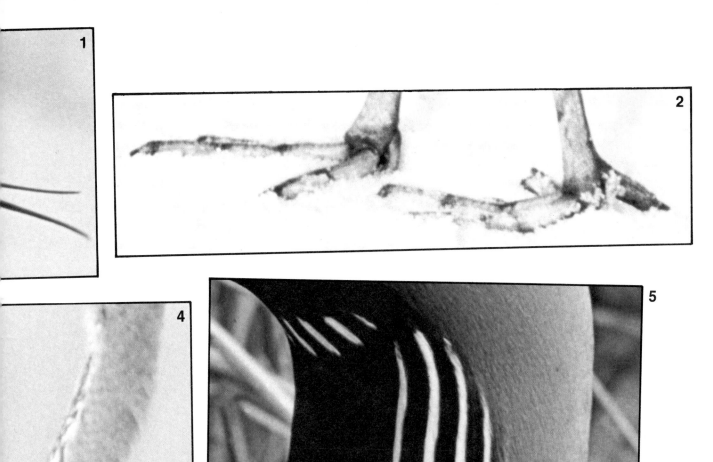

Plaster Casts of FOOTPRINTS

An observant birdwatcher always keeps an eye on the ground as well as on the sky, for a footprint may be the only sign that there is a rare bird in the area. A collection of plaster casts enables you to identify bird tracks and makes a decorative display.

Bird footprints can be found in snow, sand and mud, but unfortunately it is impossible to take casts from snow or dry sand. Prints in wet sand produce good moulds, but smooth, partly-dried mud is the best. Seashores and estuary mudflats, river banks, edges of ponds and lakes, and even partly-dried-out puddles in ploughed fields and country lanes are ideal places to find bird footprints.

The tracks you are most likely to find are those left by water birds: ducks, waders, gulls, rails and herons. Tracks of common garden birds are seen less often and are almost impossible to identify unless you see the bird making them. One way to obtain their footprints is to prepare a special area of mud in your garden.

Making plaster casts of footprints is quite simple and you need the following materials: a tin of white dental plaster of Paris which can be bought from a chemist for about 40p, a container of water, a large spoon, newspapers, paper clips, a small plastic bowl, strips of thin cardboard about 3 cm ×30 cm, a notebook and pencil.

When you find suitable tracks, make a quick sketch of the relative positions of the individual footprints and measure the distance between them as this can be useful for identification. Gently clear any loose leaves and twigs which may be covering the footprints, then select a good, clear print. Bend a strip of card into a circle big enough to surround the

print and fasten with a paper clip. Place the circle of card round the print and press down very lightly until there are no gaps at the bottom of the card. If the ground is too uneven and hard to do this, build up some loose soil around the card to block the gaps. Mix sufficient plaster of Paris in the bowl, stirring the powder into the water until the mixture is thick and creamy. Then pour it into the circle of card and smooth the top so that it is level with the edge of the card. Leave for at least 15 minutes. As the plaster sets, warmth is generated and the cast should not be moved until it is cold again. Gently lift it up and wrap it in several layers of news-

paper for safe carriage. When you return home, unwrap the cast and leave for several hours to dry out and harden. Wash the mud from it and, if necessary, use a brush to remove the last particles.

All plaster casts made in this way are negatives made from the positive footprint. They represent not the footprint, but the underside of the bird's foot which made it. To make a replica of the footprint itself, paint the surface of your original negative cast with a gelatine solution. You can make this by dissolving a small amount of powdered gelatine in hot water. Apply the solution thinly and quickly before it sets. When it is set surround your cast with cardboard and pour plaster of Paris mixture into the mould. The thin layer of gelatine will allow the new positive cast to be removed from the negative mould when it has set hard. The gelatine can be washed off with hot water.

You can make your plaster casts more attractive by painting the print and background in different colours and applying clear varnish. Coloured tape can be stuck round the edge. Write a label giving the name of the bird, the place where the print was found and the type of ground. A drawing of your rough sketch of the whole track can be included on this label.

44

● by Geoffrey Cox

British Gulls

Herring gull

This familiar gull is easily recognised by its silver-grey wings and back. In flight, the wings have black ends with white tips. The bill is yellow with a red spot on the lower mandible, the legs flesh-coloured and the eyes yellow.

The herring gull is found all round the coasts of Britain and Ireland and is increasing in numbers. There were about 334,000 pairs nesting in 1969/70.

These birds usually nest in large, noisy colonies on shingle banks, sand dunes, steep coastal slopes and wide cliff ledges. Some have taken to nesting on man-made structures, such as piers, bridges and roof-tops.

These gulls are scavengers and sometimes eat the eggs or chicks of other species. In some areas they are a serious threat to other breeding birds.

Black-headed gull

This is the smallest resident British gull. In the breeding season it is readily identified by its dark-brown head. At other times of the year the head is white with a brown smudge behind the eye. The back and wings are grey, but the white leading edges of the wings are obvious at all times of the year. Its legs and beak are red.

It is estimated that about 74,500 pairs were breeding around the coasts of Britain and Ireland in 1969/70. There are also many inland colonies; in winter they can be seen in large flocks on playing-fields, reservoirs and rubbish tips, or following the plough.

Some of the young reared in Britain cross to the Continent during their first winter, but they often return to their original colony to breed.

Common gull

This gull is not as plentiful as its name would suggest. In fact it is the least numerous of our coastal breeding gulls, with only about 12,400 pairs nesting in coastal sites in 1969/70. However, many more nest inland and most of these colonies are found in Scotland.

The common gull is similar to the herring gull, having a grey back and wings and black wing-tips with white spots, but of course it is much smaller. Its yellow-green bill is more slender than a herring gull's and its brown eyes give it a more gentle appearance.

Some of these gulls may be seen feeding on playing fields and rubbish tips, like the black-headed gull. Inland, the common gull feeds chiefly on insects, earthworms and seeds. Whereas on the coast it eats all sorts of small sea creatures as well as dead fish and refuse.

Kittiwake

A small, attractive gull, the name of which is derived from its call, the kittiwake differs from the other gulls by having triangular black wing-tips without any white marks. It also has short, black legs and a yellow bill.

The kittiwake breeds on narrow cliff-ledges. Rarely seen far from the sea, when nesting is finished, it flies out to the north Atlantic and normally avoids land. Young kittiwakes usually spend the first three years of their lives hundreds of miles from Britain, off Greenland and Newfoundland.

Kittiwakes feed mainly on small fish and other marine life. Some of the food is caught by plunging into the water, but when diving they are not as graceful as the terns. Smaller food is picked off the surface of the water.

The population of breeding kittiwakes is probably in the order of half a million pairs and there has been a steady increase since the beginning of this century. They have few natural enemies and the bird protection laws are giving them security in their growing colonies.

Great black-backed gull

The largest gull which nests in Britain, the great black-backed gull looks rather like the lesser black-backed. However, it is much larger and has a black, rather than slate-grey, back and pale flesh-coloured, not yellow, legs. It has a massive yellow beak with a red spot near the tip of the lower mandible.

These gulls will attack and kill other birds, especially if the prey is slow or clumsy on land. The great black-backed often eats young birds and on Skokholm Island, Pembrokeshire, in 1958, great black-backed gulls killed 2536 Manx shearwaters as well as a number of puffins.

This species nests in the west and north of Britain and about 22,000 pairs nested in 1969/70.

Lesser black-backed gull

This bird is similar in size to the herring gull. However, the back and wings are a much darker shade of grey and its general appearance is that of a more powerfully built gull. Its legs are yellow.

The lesser black-backed gull is a migratory species and in winter reaches Portugal, Spain and north-west Africa, though there is evidence that more birds are over-wintering in this country.

These gulls nest in large, often dense colonies on rocky islands or sand dunes near the sea, on moorland or on islands in lakes away from the sea.

Colonies of lesser black-backed gulls are scattered around the coasts of Britain and Ireland and in 1969/70 the breeding population was nearly 47,000 pairs.

● *by Peter Holden*

45

COMMON GULL

KITTIWAKE

LESSER BLACK-BACKED
GULL

46

British Gulls

HERRING GULL

Winter

BLACK-HEADED
GULL

GREAT BLACK-BACKED
GULL

Summer

47

STARLINGS

A flock of quarrelsome, ugly starlings hardly evokes enthusiasm in a birdwatcher, and it is very easy to neglect our common birds and only concentrate on 'another tick' for our bird list. Common birds make excellent subjects for projects because they are so numerous and widespread.

Starlings are not protected birds as at times they can be serious pests. They eat the young shoots of cereal crops, and grain put out for chickens and pheasants, and cause serious damage in fruit-growing areas by eating cherries, apples, pears and soft fruit. On the other hand, during the breeding season they feed mainly on insects, many of which are pests to agriculture and forestry. Starlings can be a great nuisance; in towns they foul pavements and window ledges and cause damage to buildings; in plantations the sheer weight of their numbers can seriously damage the trees.

The starling perhaps more than any other bird deserves the title 'common'. There may be as many as 10,000,000 in this coun-

David and Katie Urry

try, which places it among the five most abundant British land birds. It can also be described common in another sense, in that its habits to us are rather coarse and vulgar.

The birds often have an un-

tidy appearance and walk with an ungainly waddle. They are most often seen in groups which are noisy and quarrelsome. People who feed the birds in their gardens often accuse the starling of being a greedy bird, for scraps thrown onto the lawn or bird table will soon disappear when spotted by the local starlings. They are far from dainty eaters, swallowing large pieces of food whole or carrying them away, and they often drive away the smaller birds. All these things combined give the starling a character which few people find attractive.

This was how I always regarded starlings until, by chance, three young birds came into my possession. I then discovered how interesting they could be. I kept the small grey-brown birds in a large metal wastepaper basket, lined with newspaper and covered with wire netting. When I took charge of them they were old enough to have learnt to recognise their parents, and would therefore not take food from humans. I had to force feed them, pushing small pellets of bread mixed with milk and beaten egg into their beaks which were held open by a friend. But within two days they were clammering for food whenever I approached, and took it readily from my fingers.

I had read that young birds accepted the first living things that they saw as their parents; and I was surprised to find at this rather late stage they forgot their two parents and adopted me as substitute. I fed them at hourly intervals but this still did not keep them quiet and their constant shrill squawking eventually drove me from my room to seek quieter haunts; the birds had taken over!

The biggest, most forward, and I assumed the oldest, was the first to develop each new antic in starling behaviour. For example,

● *by Geoffrey Cox*

E. A. Janes

it was the first to learn to drink. When I gave the birds a dish of water, they only paddled in it, flicking it over themselves with their beaks and wings. The oldest bird suddenly, almost by accident, found itself with the water in its beak, then raised its head and swallowed – the following day all three birds were drinking.

The most interesting habit that the birds developed was the typical feeding action of the starling. This can easily be seen when starlings are feeding on a lawn. The birds push their closed bills into the turf and then open them taught the birds this special trick. Of course the birds had needed no tuition, as this is instinct – a habit which develops naturally. The birds could definitely not have copied their parents, and they had certainly never seen me performing these antics!

The birds were soon ready to be released, and I put their makeshift home by an open window. At first they took very short flights and returned to the window ledge. Eventually they flew right away and I thought this would be the last I was to see of them. However, they still returned. I decided that activities practised by many birds and are probably most frequently observed in starlings. Birds generally sun-bathe by perching on the ground or on a rooftop, and spreading their wings and tails. Anting takes place in the summer when the insects are active. The birds pick up ants and push them into their feathers, often rubbing them along the length of the wing feathers. During this time they take on very awkward and comical-looking poses and appear to get a strange, excited enjoyment from the activity as if they are being tickled.

to force the grass blades and roots apart, and to open up the shallow burrows of worms and insect larvae. The first sign of this activity in my birds was a pecking at the newspaper lining their improvised home. I then decided it was time to encourage the birds to feed in the proper manner. I placed some worms and centipedes, with which I was now varying their diet, in the palm of my hand, covering them with the fingers of the other hand upon which one of the starlings was perched. I watched the bird push its beak between two fingers and then open it, forcing my fingers apart and disclosing the food below. It picked up a piece of food and swallowed it.

I now fed the birds regularly in this way. Friends thought I had I would have to release the birds away from my room. I carried the birds, perched on my arm, some distance and put them on the ground. As they began to search for food in the grass, I tiptoed away. I had not gone many paces before there was a fluttering behind me and three young starlings settled one on each shoulder and the third on my head. The sight of this strange behaviour almost caused a passerby to fall off his bicycle! Eventually I managed to leave the birds in a small copse, and after this I saw nothing of them.

My experience with these young birds gave me a particular interest in starlings and I have since become aware of many other interesting features in their behaviour. Sun-bathing and 'anting' are I also discovered that starlings produce pellets, and actually watched a bird eject one. It was about an inch and a quarter long, pointed at one end and composed of hard outer cases of beetles or other insects.

It is hardly necessary to attract starlings into gardens; they come of their own accord, and most people are concerned far more with keeping them away. However, a group of starlings can bring as much interest to small urban gardens as a flock of great tits or blue tits bring to a larger suburban one. Lawns and grassy areas are their favourite feeding grounds and in winter they will come to feed on almost any kitchen scraps or food that you put out for the other birds.

The great grey owl is one of the largest of all owls and its cold, steely stare makes it quite unnerving. Great greys do not live in Britain but are found in the northern regions of Europe and North America. They make their homes in the dense pine forest often using the abandoned nests of birds of prey.

The kestrel on the crane

As towns and industrial centres spread into the surrounding countryside, many wild creatures are being forced to relinquish their traditional homes. Fields, woods, hedges and marshes are engulfed by brick and cement. Even cliffs and gulleys, once inaccessible because of their distance from towns, are no longer safe places for wildlife. Easy transport and the popularity of rock-climbing and hill-walking have made many of these spots unsuitable for some of the more timid creatures.

However, nature will not be beaten so easily. Observers note that many birds and beasts are rehabilitating themselves. Kittiwakes, which are sea-cliff dwellers, have nested on the ledges of warehouses by the river. The rare black redstart has nested in the ruins of bombed houses in London. Hares find that airfields are safe abodes and they nonchalantly watch the comings and goings of the aircraft. One nesting season, much of my time was spent in searching for the nest of the kestrel, that lovely little falcon which is commonly seen hovering over the fields and hedges as it hunts for mice. I failed to find one until a birdwatching friend, who is employed in a famous shipyard, told me of a pair nesting in a huge tower crane there!

First I had to get permission to investigate this report, and to my surprise and delight was given every assistance. I had hardly hoped that the builders of great ships would bother about birds' nests but the results speak for themselves.

The nest was situated on a girder, underneath the machine room on the swinging boom of the crane, with a sheer drop of approximately 140 feet to the ground. Originally, this nest had been built by a pair of rooks, who seemed to have decided to compete with the human builders below for engineering honours! They built their nest almost entirely of wire—pieces of cable, packing-case wire, and welding wires. Some of their ends were so securely bound round the girders that nothing short of an earthquake would shift them. See how adaptable nature is!

When I arrived, the hen kestrel was sitting fairly tightly. It was possible to walk along the catwalk within eight feet of her before she left her nest, when she would fly around the crane and swoop at me trying to scare me away. She took to my "hide" quickly and, as I expected, the click of my camera shutter meant nothing to her. She

was too used to the noise and clamour of the yard to bother with such a triviality.

Normally, when I am birdwatching I am more used to the sighing of the wind through the heather and the plaintive cries of moorland birds. I found the grinding crash of the huge gears in the machine room behind me almost unbearable, but the kestrel brooded her eggs without concern. The great crane lifted tons of prefabricated sections, swung slowly round and dropped them into position. The huge hulk of the ship below acquired a set of ribs and a prow, but the kestrel thought nothing of these marvels—she had eggs to hatch. Eventually, she successfully hatched five of her six eggs and, sensibly, she allowed the sixth to lie among her powder-puff chicks. When they were very small, she brooded the chicks to keep them warm and displayed a tenderness towards them that surprised most people. This strong maternal instinct seems even stranger in a predatory bird when you know something of its life history. Here is an extract from my notebook which recorded the minute-by-minute events at the nest and illustrates a "domestic scene".

"The cock kestrel calls from a short distance, an insistent sound like a creaking gate. The hen, brooding her restless down-covered chicks, replies in a rather thinner, higher-pitched version of his call and raises her head feathers. They carry on a sort of conversation which might almost be, "I have a mouse!" "High time, too—the children are hungry." She leaves the nest and returns in a moment with a small mouse in her beak.

"The nestlings are very excited and she stands well back from them, clutching her prey in her strong talons, and begins to tear small pieces from it. With her head to one side, she delicately offers a piece to each chick and one by one feeds them, giving them the soft pieces only, fur and all; she eats the coarse or bony pieces herself.

"One by one, the nestlings drop back satisfied and close their eyes as she stands watch over them. Meanwhile, the crane, still working and swinging, has turned, so that the sun beats down on the nest. The hen tries to shelter her brood from its rays, but now her family is proving more than a wingful. She droops her wings and straddles the chicks as they jostle and push for a place in the shade; she pants in the heat."

by James Alder ●

Soon, however, as the nestlings grew strong and their rust-brown barred feathers pushed through their baby down, the hen joined her mate in search for food. Many a young riverside rat or dockyard mouse ended its life in her talons and sometimes it was the fate of the more innocent sparrows.

The once tidy wire nest became foul-smelling and infested with blue-bottles, which the young kestrels pursued and ate with obvious enjoyment. They clasped the wire strands with their sharp claws as they exercised their growing wings and played a sort of game of tig along the girders, panicking wildly if they lost balance and rushing back to the security of the nest platform to recover their nerve. They preened their plumage carefully to remove the irksome down and, as if to exercise their eyes that would one day detect the movement of a beetle from two hundred feet up, they intently watched the loose feathers that idled in the air currents above the girders. Then came a day when the parents would not return to the nest: when all they did was to call from a nearby crane. What were they saying? "Here, I have a mouse for you, if you come and get it!" I watched the first youngster launch himself into the vastness below him. He dropped and teetered on the air uncertainly, and then, triumphantly, his winnowing wings and frantic ruddering won him control and he was flying, to circle the crane and land on the platform near me.

My last view of the kestrel family was of the second eldest sitting on the girder apparently contemplating the plunge which he was soon to make and the others appearing somewhat glum. Birds do get nerves about their first "solo" you know! One of the fledglings made a bad job of his first flight and landed in a pool of bilge oil. He came into my possession and I cleaned him and trained him to hunt. Eventually, he was released back into the wild.

But that's another story!

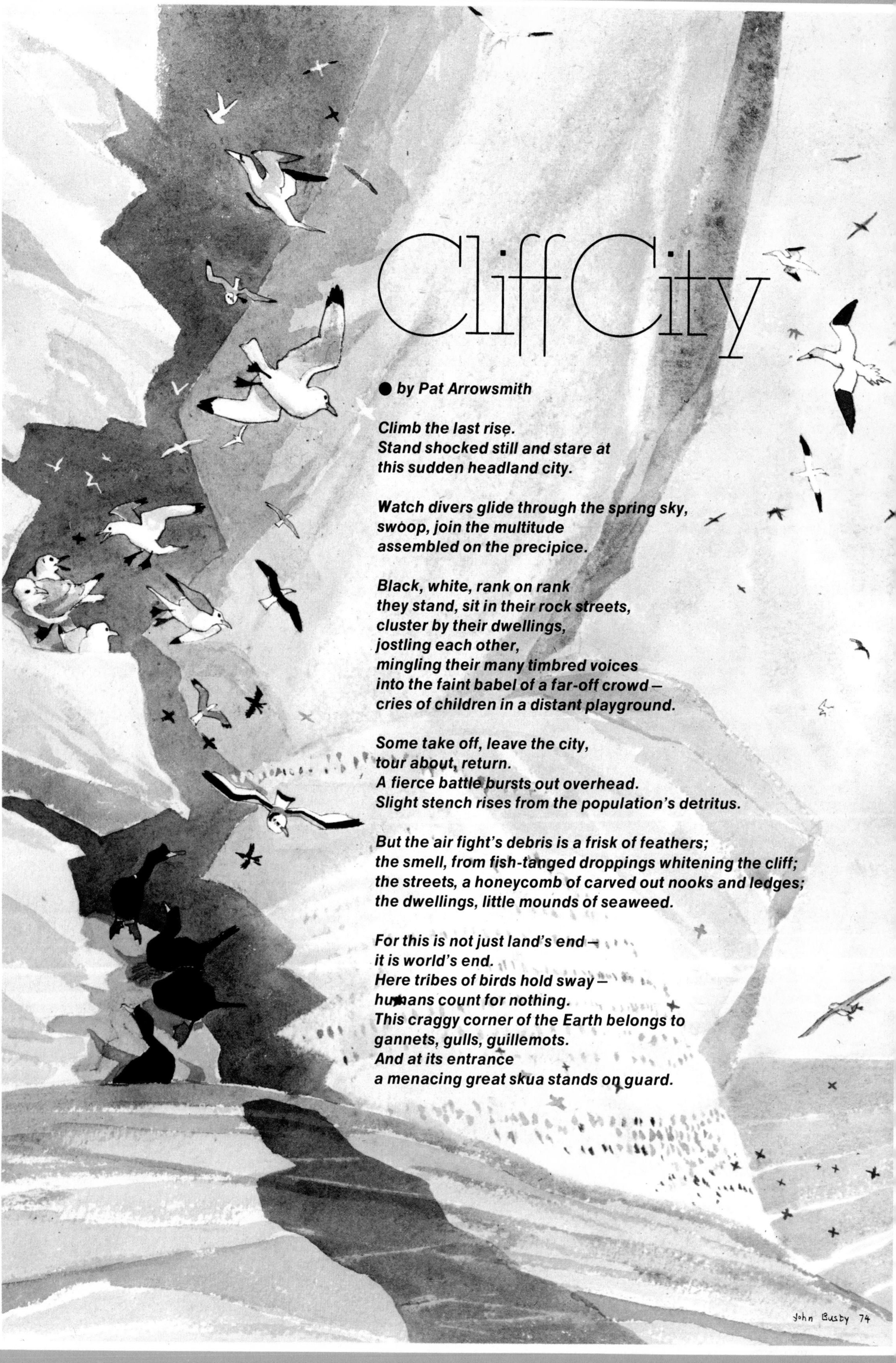

Cliff City

● by Pat Arrowsmith

Climb the last rise.
Stand shocked still and stare at
this sudden headland city.

Watch divers glide through the spring sky,
swoop, join the multitude
assembled on the precipice.

Black, white, rank on rank
they stand, sit in their rock streets,
cluster by their dwellings,
jostling each other,
mingling their many timbred voices
into the faint babel of a far-off crowd —
cries of children in a distant playground.

Some take off, leave the city,
tour about, return.
A fierce battle bursts out overhead.
Slight stench rises from the population's detritus.

But the air fight's debris is a frisk of feathers;
the smell, from fish-tanged droppings whitening the cliff;
the streets, a honeycomb of carved out nooks and ledges;
the dwellings, little mounds of seaweed.

For this is not just land's end —
it is world's end.
Here tribes of birds hold sway —
humans count for nothing.
This craggy corner of the Earth belongs to
gannets, gulls, guillemots.
And at its entrance
a menacing great skua stands on guard.

John Busby 74

BIRD

PELLETS

Bird pellets, or castings, consist of hard, undigested material which is of little food value to the bird. The bones of birds, mammals and fishes; teeth, claws and beaks; tough outer casings of insects; seed husks are just a few of the

Tawny Owl

items found. These hard parts are usually packed together with softer substances like mammal fur, bird feathers and vegetable matter.

Which birds produce pellets?

More species eject pellets than many birdwatchers realise. Over 330 species are mentioned in bird books and papers. Birds producing pellets in this country include: common garden species like the robin, dunnock and starling; waterside feeders like the heron, kingfisher and herring gull; farmland birds such as the rook, carrion crow

● *by David Glue*

Heron

Udo Hirsch

55

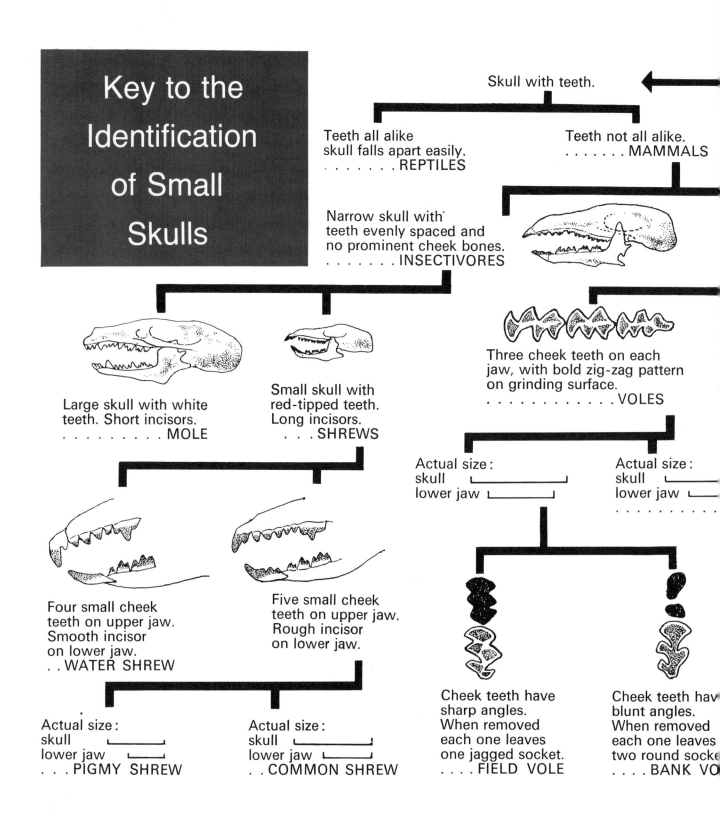

Key to the Identification of Small Skulls

Skull with teeth.

Teeth all alike skull falls apart easily.
. . . . .REPTILES

Teeth not all alike.
. . . . . . .MAMMALS

Narrow skull with teeth evenly spaced and no prominent cheek bones.
. . . . INSECTIVORES

Three cheek teeth on each jaw, with bold zig-zag pattern on grinding surface.
. . . . VOLES

Large skull with white teeth. Short incisors.
. . . . MOLE

Small skull with red-tipped teeth. Long incisors.
. . . SHREWS

Actual size:
skull
lower jaw
. . . .

Actual size:
skull
lower jaw

Four small cheek teeth on upper jaw. Smooth incisor on lower jaw.
. . WATER SHREW

Five small cheek teeth on upper jaw. Rough incisor on lower jaw.

Cheek teeth have sharp angles. When removed each one leaves one jagged socket.
. . . . FIELD VOLE

Cheek teeth have blunt angles. When removed each one leaves two round socke
. . . . BANK VO

Actual size:
skull
lower jaw
. . . PIGMY SHREW

Actual size:
skull
lower jaw
. . COMMON SHREW

and yellowhammer; and predators like the shrikes, owls, falcons and hawks.

Which pellets are worth collecting?

Pellets can give valuable clues about the foods eaten. The identification of the undigested food is often difficult, but certain species eject pellets that are both easier to collect and to analyse.

Larger birds which roost communally or regularly in one spot produce the most useful pellets. Gull, crow and wader pellets can be found quite easily, but it is the birds of prey which are the most helpful, particularly the owls.

Where does one collect pellets?

A careful search of the ground in the following places will frequently prove successful: nest-

sites for heron, barn owl and rook pellets; roosts for curlew, little owl and herring-gull pellets; feeding vantage points for peregrine falcon, great grey shrike, kingfisher and spotted flycatcher pellets.

With many species, searching for pellets is a time-consuming business, but once the "pellet stations" have been located, you can collect material regularly.

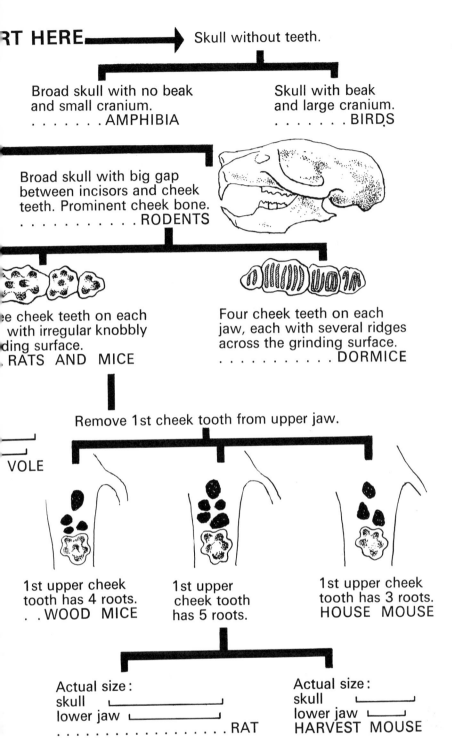

RT HERE ⟶ Skull without teeth.

Broad skull with no beak and small cranium.
. . . . . . .AMPHIBIA

Skull with beak and large cranium.
. . . . BIRDS

Broad skull with big gap between incisors and cheek teeth. Prominent cheek bone.
. . . . .RODENTS

e cheek teeth on each with irregular knobbly ding surface.
. RATS AND MICE

Four cheek teeth on each jaw, each with several ridges across the grinding surface.
. . . . .DORMICE

Remove 1st cheek tooth from upper jaw.

VOLE

1st upper cheek tooth has 4 roots.
. .WOOD MICE

1st upper cheek tooth has 5 roots.

1st upper cheek tooth has 3 roots.
HOUSE MOUSE

Actual size:
skull |____|
lower jaw |_____|
. . . . .RAT

Actual size:
skull |___|
lower jaw |___|
HARVEST MOUSE

Copyright: Dr. P. Morris (Mammal Society) and Mr. D. Glue (British Trust for Ornithology).

Barn owls roosting and breeding in farm outbuildings, for instance, will use the same spot for months, even years, if they are not disturbed, while great grey shrikes may return to the same winter territory and use the same vantage point annually.

Dissecting pellets

By carefully dissecting a pellet you can discover what the bird had been eating. You will the need the following things:

a dish containing warm water,
a pair of mounted needles,
a soft paint brush,
tweezers or forceps,
blotting paper.

The pellet should be soaked in warm water for about half an hour, then gently teased apart. Each bone, skull, beetle wing, or other item should be removed carefully and cleaned with a soft paintbrush. They should be washed and then dried with blotting paper.

Analysing pellets

Try to identify all the hard and soft parts; a hand lens is helpful. For the skulls of small mammals use the key opposite. The following books, which you can get from your local library, are also useful: **The Handbook of British Mammals** by H N Southern (Blackwell), **Mammals of Britain, their Tracks, Trails and Signs** by Lawrence and Brown (Blandford), **The Oxford Book of Insects** by J Burton (OUP) and **Beetles of the British Isles** by E R Linsen (Warne).

The ability to digest harder parts of food varies considerably among different birds. Heron pellets, for instance, appear to be composed of little more than masses of compressed fur, but the fish bones and mammal teeth within tell tales. Diurnal birds of prey like the kestrel, sparrowhawk and golden eagle, which have strong neck muscles, tear at the flesh, eating only parts of it and breaking some bones, so that pellets only contain small pieces. The owls are more helpful; their ability to digest bones is poor and they do not normally decapitate their prey, so a whole skull may be found in their pellets.

Displaying pellet contents

Arrange all the hard pieces found on a sheet of card and stick them in place with strong glue. Beside each of the identifiable remains write the name of the animal or plant from which it came. On the top of the card write the name of the bird which produced the pellet, the date and the place where it was collected. The soft material should be put into a small, polythene bag and labelled.

The collection, dissection and identification of pellets can make a fascinating study and give a useful indication of birds' diets.

The dipper

Out of the water the dipper looks like a portly diner with a clean bib tucked into his collar, but once the bird plunges through the surface it is transformed into a slim, silvery creature, twisting through the water as it looks for food. The water, being denser than air, compresses the bird and the many air bubbles trapped among the feathers make its plumage glisten.

Dippers feed under the water, turning over small stones to look for freshwater shrimps, insect larvae and snails. They may stay underwater for up to half a minute, but most submersions last between 10 and 20 seconds.

Dippers are found by fast-flowing streams and are resident in Britain, being particularly common in south-west and north England, Wales and Scotland. They are also found in Ireland and in many parts of Europe.

How
to
draw
birds

One of the best ways of recording the details of a bird in the wild is with a quick sketch. With practice, even the least talented of us can manage a rough field drawing.

To draw a bird you must understand its basic anatomy. In its simplest form a bird consists of two egg-shaped masses of bone and muscle—the head and body—joined by a flexible neck. Far too many bird drawings are incorrect because no allowance is made for the length of the neck (see figs. 1 and 2).

1. Correct

2. Incorrect (no neck)

Always sketch these two masses first (fig. 3). Next indicate the position of the wings, the angle of the tail and the placing of the legs (fig. 4). Draw in the outline of

6. Proportions and placings

the feathers (fig. 5) and you have a field sketch. Figure 6 shows the different proportions and placings

of the head and body outlines for different species.

If you are using your diagram for identification, label the distinguishing points (fig. 7). This will help you recognise the bird in your field guide.

The more competent artist will want to draw detailed pictures, and the best way to tackle this is to closely examine dead specimens. If you find any dead birds take them home and carefully study the colour, the way the feathers lie and the way the wings move. Draw the bird at various angles and in several postures. From these detailed diagrams and your rough sketches drawn in the field showing movement of the bird, you can compose a complete picture.

You do not have to be an excellent artist to produce a picture of a bird, the collage (left) of a great spotted woodpecker by John Paige is made from pieces of newspaper. Collages can be made from any material—string, seeds, felt, feathers, leaves to name but a few. The more varied the medium the more interesting the picture.

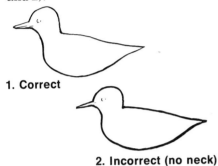

3. Head and body outlines

4. Head and body outlines with positions of beak, eye, wings, tail and legs indicated

5. Head and body outlines with feather masses filled in

7. Distinguishing points

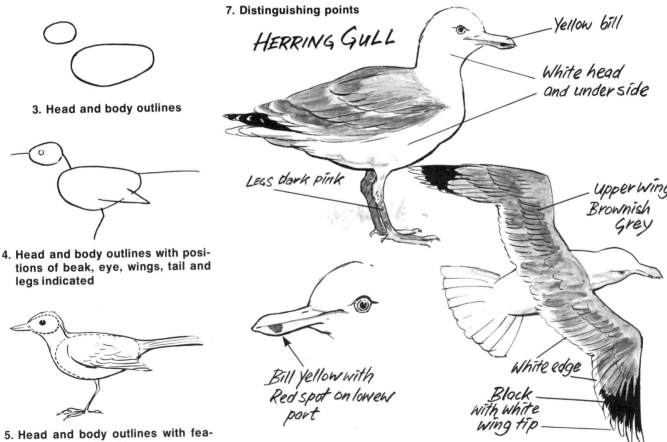

HERRING GULL

Yellow bill

White head and underside

Upper wing Brownish Grey

Legs dark pink

Bill yellow with Red spot on lower part

White edge

Black with white wing tip

● **by P. H. T. Hartley**

61

A birdwatcher often needs to estimate the size of flocks for studies on bird populations. If the numbers are small—a dozen or so—there is little problem, as the individual birds can be counted. If the numbers are much larger, it is quite impossible to count each bird, particularly if they are flying. So you have to adopt a method of estimating the number. The usual way is to quickly count part of the flock (say 10, 20 or 50, depending on the size and how fast they are moving) and then estimate what proportion this is of the total number. For example, if you see a flock flying over and quickly count a group of 20 of them, then reckon this forms one-tenth of the whole flock—the answer is approximately 200 birds. One point to remember, do not become so engrossed in counting the birds that you fail to identify them!

Of course, this is easier said than done and needs plenty of practice, but after a while your estimates should become more accurate. You may then ask, how do you know if your estimates are near the correct number and if you are improving?

Firstly, if you see a stationary flock, such as gulls on a ploughed field, you can make your quick estimate and then actually count the individuals in the whole flock. You will then see how near you were to the correct answer.

Secondly, whenever you see a photograph of a large number of birds in a book or in a newspaper, make your estimate in the usual way and then check by counting.

Thirdly, you can practise with objects other than birds. Throw down onto a table a handful of rice, peanuts or marbles. Estimate the number and then check by counting.

When practising in this way, make your estimate in a few seconds (you cannot expect a flock of birds to stay still for five minutes while you count them). Also, each time, write down your first number and then the correct figure. Apart from seeing your progress, you will probably notice that you have a tendency to either over-estimate each time or to under-estimate; you should allow for this tendency in your future counts. After a bit of practice you will become quite accurate, and it will help you a great deal in your studies of bird numbers.

How good are you at estimating the number of birds in a large flock? Look at the photograph above for five seconds. How many birds are there? Now count them and see how near you were to the correct answer.

Estimating Bird Flocks

A Peaceful Evening

After carefully examining my camera, and assuring myself that the roll of film which I had purchased the day before was indeed intact, I made myself more comfortable behind an elder bush. I was sitting concealed in a tunnel of foliage that covered a slight bend in the stream. As I waited, camera at the ready, rays of sunlight slowly began to filter through the leaves and play on the rippling surface of the stream. I had not been waiting very long when a small dark shape flitted between the long spoke-like branches of the elder on the opposite bank. It was a robin. Silently, the robin flew down to a rock in the stream. For an instant the sun vanished and a horse cantered noisily past in the field behind.

The robin flew back to his tree and then returned, with the sun, to his stone in the stream. With a jerk of his tail he hopped bravely into the glistening water, seemingly unaware of my presence. Quickly, he came back to his stony perch and stared at the water, then slowly, very slowly, raised his head until his beady eye glared directly at me. Without a sound he turned his back on me, hopped into the stream and proceeded to wash and enjoy himself—it was evident that enjoyment was foremost in his mind. Again and again he hopped back into the stream after a brief preen on the wet stone. At last he tired of the water and, with a good shake, he chose the topmost branch in the sunlight and began once again to sort out his feathers. He was but a quivering shadow to look at with the brilliant sunshine behind.

Robin

Gordon Langsbury

A raucous 'caw' rent the air above me and the ivy rustled as a magpie landed in the dead tree beside me. The robin hurriedly flew away. In a few bounding leaps, accompanied by much noise, the magpie arrived at the water's

Chaffinch

edge, apparently for a drink. However, just as his beak was in the water he caught sight of me. With an unbelievable squawk of frustration he rose on his stubby wings and flew from sight.

As the magpie left I saw, down the same stream, a thrush eating purple berries. A chaffinch came looking, it seemed, for a lost mate; it called incessantly and then left. I was glad to be rid of the monotonous sound. A pair of coal tits appeared on the scene; they were even smaller than the blue tits that arrived shortly after. They played for a while and moved on. The sun disappeared behind some clouds; a twittering flock of goldfinches passed overhead. It was time I left. I had not taken any pictures at all!

● **Paul O'Nolan** (Y.O.C. Member)

1

2

Matin

3

4

5

6

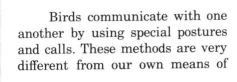

The
g Game

Birds communicate with one another by using special postures and calls. These methods are very different from our own means of communication. For example, we have specific facial expressions to show anger or happiness. Birds, however, show these different moods by erecting certain feathers and adopting certain positions. This series of photographs shows the courtship display of the black-headed gull.

A male calls for a mate (1) and warns off other males in the vicinity (2, 3 & 4). The female then arrives in his territory and has to win his confidence. She does this by running along with him with head down (5) and by turning away, so her black head and bill do not show (6). These are called submissive gestures. The courtship ceremony ends with the male and female mating (7).

● photographed by Udo Hirsch

A–E

Oystercatchers usually nest in fields or on shingle, but this pair chose the cavity at the top of a fence-post beside the main Kilmarnock to Glasgow road.

A PILLAR TO NEST ON

● *photographed by William S Paton*

AVOCET

In the early 1790s, Havergate Island was used by smugglers. An old cattleman and his wife lived in a cottage on the island until about 1935. For a further four years, bullocks, horses and sheep grazed on the island's marshes, but the livestock was removed in 1939 as the river banks were being damaged. War then broke out and no one was very interested in the island, except perhaps the odd wildfowler.

In 1947 two people, who were staying at the hotel at Orford, decided to stroll along the main river bank. After walking for about two miles, they were very surprised to see avocets fly overhead. With great interest they watched where the birds went — across the river and over to Havergate. Fortunately both these people were keen birdwatchers and immediately recognised the birds — you can imagine their excitement! Wanting to investigate further, they hired a rowing boat and arriving on the island, they were delighted to discover that the avocets were

nesting. This set the ball rolling and the RSPB quickly arranged a rota of voluntary watchers to guard the nest-site.

The following year, the RSPB purchased Havergate Island in order to improve the area for the avocets. Sluices were replaced and river banks rebuilt. In many places the banks were a complete honeycomb of rabbit burrows. Lagoons and islands were formed by flooding various areas — the lagoons providing the feeding areas and the island the nesting sites. It took a great deal of hard work to make the island a suitable habitat.

In these early years very few young avocets were reared. Then, in 1953, came the dramatic flooding of the east coast. At Havergate there were 16 large breaks in the river banks and one sluice was washed out completely. The reserve looked like a reservoir. It was obvious that with only one small sluice left we were not going to have the island drained in time for the avocets' return that spring. So

six pumps were hired and kept running night and day by a local garage owner and myself working round-the-clock shifts.

It was tiring work, but it was worth it in the end. As the first avocets arrived in early March, there was just enough land above water. As well as the draining, repair work had to be carried out on the breaks in the river walls. With the local people's help, mud-filled sacks and large wooden poles were packed into the holes. Gradually all the breaks were filled and the avocets could nest in safety for that season. I remember that this work came to a fitting end when, as the last break was completed, one of the working party picked up a piece of driftwood and wrote in the mud in large letters, 'Welcome back avocets 1953'. During that season 45 pairs nested.

By 1958 the number of breeding pairs was up to about 90, but from these only 30 young were successfully fledged. Black-headed gulls were found to be the main

● by Reg Partridge

danger, so various methods of control were tried. After six attempts, the seventh method of raking their nests early on in the breeding season finally proved successful.

Although black-headed gulls and the weather have been the two main obstructions to success, there have always been others. In the early days, rats had to be dealt with, while nowadays stoats and weasels are rather troublesome. Large gulls are not free from blame either, particularly the lesser black-backed gull.

With the successful control of the gulls there has been an encouraging increase in the number of young avocets fledged. In 1969 184 young were reared, in 1970 there was a slight decrease with 178 young, but in 1971 we suffered yet another setback, rearing only 103 young. The main reasons for this were the poor weather conditions that summer.

In most years the first avocets are sighted in early March. Straight away the fighting and chasing begins and the noise level on the island rises considerably. This is all part of their courtship and display behaviour, and mating soon follows. Next, the pairs start scraping hollows in the ground, and the final nest-site is chosen by about mid-April.

The avocet's nest is a shallow scrape in the bare mud or short vegetation. It is lined with dead grasses or weeds which the birds find washed up along the water's edge. The nests on Havergate Island have to be checked regularly, as they are often close to the water and can easily be flooded in heavy rain. I have occasionally had to take a shovel and build up some mud around the nest. It is always interesting to see how easily the avocets accept this; one can almost imagine the relief they feel.

The incubation takes about 23 days, and the nesting season is spread through May into June, according to how late the season or how great the losses. The first chicks are seen by about mid-May and it is this period that causes the most concern. However, the end of June, when the first young avocets are seen on the wing, is the period everyone has been waiting for.

The avocet's diet is varied, fly and beetle larvae, small, shrimp-like animals and fish spawn are all eaten occasionally. The availability of food is, of course, affected by the weather, and as summer approaches and it becomes warmer, the food in the water and the mud becomes more plentiful. An avocet feeds by sweeping its bill from left and right through the shallow water and on top of the mud. There are occasions when it will feed in deep water, sweeping its bill through the water or soft mud in one direction only. At the end of the season it is fascinating to watch several feeding together. Perhaps 20 will be seen moving through the water in a pack, then with a quick about-turn they will dash back over the same ground, obviously having found a good feeding patch.

In winter, when most of the avocets have departed (one or two will occasionally winter at Havergate), the management work on the reserve starts. The hides, or perhaps a sluice, will need repair but usually it is the river banks that require most of the attention. Heavy seas may have washed out some of the stones and it is essential that these are replaced as soon as possible.

Looking back, we have been able to make quite a few changes to the island's marshland habitat. We have provided more ground for the avocets to nest and rear their chicks, and the RSPB's research department is studying the problem of food shortage. For the future there is still more management work to be carried out on various areas of the island, so even more avocets will be able to breed.

Jan Van de Kam

Whose Bill?

One winter Dago, Dusky Girl and their two cygnets only appeared on Swan Lake on 16 and 22 November. That's funny because they know the place well—probably as well as Fuzzy and Muzzy who set up the record for the longest stay; they came to Swan Lake every single day between 26 November and 22 March.

Dago, Dusky Girl, Fuzzy and Muzzy *must* be swans. But how can we know such intimate details as their individual activities? Obviously they have been marked in some way—and so they have, not by human devices, but 'as nature intended'. These are not mute swans, such as those to be found on nearly every stretch of river, or park lake in Britain, but Bewick's swans, smaller birds that migrate from Siberia, where they breed. Each Bewick's swan has a black and yellow bill, and the pattern on each bill is different for every single bird.

At Slimbridge these swans have been encouraged to fly up every day from the Severn estuary to what has inevitably become known as Swan Lake. This is a small pond within the Wildfowl Trust, flanked on one side by Peter Scott's house and large studio window and on the other by an office block. Prior to 1964, small numbers of wild Bewick's swans wintered on the Severn. However, in the spring of that year Swan Lake was closed to the public and some grain was scattered around. The wild Bewicks' were attracted by the calls of those in the collection and soon were quite at home on the lake.

That year twenty-four swans were identified by their bill patterns and given names. Each bill pattern was drawn and the bird allocated a file which contained all the information known about it,

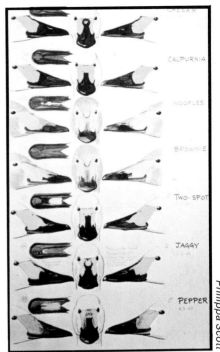

Philippa Scott

Each bird is given a name and "identikit" drawings are kept on file, together with detailed information and photographs.

Philippa Scott

C. R. Knights (Ardea)

● *by Mary E. Evans*

together with photographs. In the autumn, some of the twenty-four returned and with them many strangers. Each year the numbers built up, so that in the peak year so far, 1970-71, 626 different swans came to Swan Lake. Of course, they were not all there on the same day. The maximum on the pond at one time has been 411.

The swans are all given names as these can be associated in pairs, and are so much easier to remember than numbers. There are now over 2000 individuals on the files. This offers a great opportunity to study their family lives: what age do they mate at, breed at, how many cygnets do they have? For example, it seems that these birds never divorce, but are loyal to their partner.

Not only do the swans look different, but they may have different temperaments. Some are aggressive, some are timid, especially when Bill Shakespear appears with the food barrow. He alone is allowed outside with the swans, and they, for their part, recognise him. They are much more wary of the person who has to feed them on Bill's day off.

The public view the swans at one corner of the pond, and the Trust members from an observatory. At night the pond is floodlit and there is the breathtaking spectacle of the swans flying out to the river estuary for the night; others remain on the pond—drifting serenely around.

Every day a register is taken, so newcomers can be noted as soon as they arrive. Those that have visited Slimbridge in previous winters breeze in as if they had never been away. Real newcomers are far less cofident. They must wonder why so many birds want to crowd together on this one small pond! Some of the swans do not attend every day—they may feed elsewhere, depending on the weather. Each winter we attempt to catch some of the swans by means of a screened waterway in one corner of the pond. Here food is put daily, and, every so often, when a good number of swans are feeding there, someone gently drives them

into a holding pen. There they are put into special green, plastic jackets so that they can neither flap their wings nor walk off—protection for both ourselves and the swans!

Each swan is ringed, weighed and measured. For three winters they also had their wing tips and tails dyed yellow, so that they could easily be noticed when they were away from Slimbridge. We heard several amusing 'explanations' of the dye from visitors. "It's the males that have yellow tails; the females are all white," for example! The birds were dyed firstly, to try and find out where they went during the winter, when they were absent from Slimbridge, and secondly, to map their migration route between here and Siberia, a distance of 2600 miles. In fact these questions overlap considerably; a number of swans when they disappear from Slimbridge, even in the middle of winter, start back on their migration to the Netherlands or Germany. We imagined that they simply stayed in some part of England which, of course, some of them do.

The swans are also x-rayed, and, to our horror, we find that over a third contain lead pellets—a shocking reflection on so-called sportsmen, as these birds are protected throughout their range.

Special metal rings, with a number and an address, are put on one leg, so that anyone finding a dead bird will know where to send the information. On the other leg we put a plastic ring with large numbers that can be read at a distance through binoculars or a telescope. Thus, birdwatchers who are not experts on the bill patterns can recognise our birds when away from Slimbridge.

Unringed birds, are, of course, just Tom, Dick and Harry to an untrained eye, and so three excursions have been made to follow the swans on part of their migration. For instance in March 1972 Dafila Scott and I went first to the Netherlands, and near Nijkerk saw ten Slimbridge swans out of a total of 204. Among them was a

pair called Peasant and Gypsy and their two cygnets. They have been coming to Slimbridge for the past six winters, and Dafila had seen them two years previously on migration in the Netherlands. The amazing thing was that Peasant, Gypsy and their two cygnets, and Dafila and I decided to travel to exactly the same spot in Germany during exactly the same four days. There on the Elbe estuary, northwest of Hamburg, among 950 swans in the area were the two familiar faces! Ten other Slimbridge swans were also there.

After that, the farther northeast the swans go, the less we know of their movements. Perhaps communications are not so good. Certainly there are not so many people to spot them as they reach their breeding grounds, where they are supposed to return to the same nest site each summer. This is perhaps where pairs that have become accidentally separated meet up again. Indeed Fuzzy and Muzzy were such a pair. In 1970-71 Muzzy arrived and spent a lonely winter by herself. On 14 February Fuzzy turned up to be her only Valentine, but too late—Muzzy had not been able to wait that long and had departed twelve days earlier. Fuzzy hung around hopefully until 22 March, but on that day Dafila Scott had seen Muzzy on migration in Denmark. However, the following winter they promptly returned together, a day after the first Bewick's arrived in the area.

Lancelot is now the most experienced Slimbridge-Siberia commuter. He is the only one returning out of the veteran 24 campaigners, and has now spent twelve consecutive winters at Slimbridge. This is exciting and rather flattering!

Many visitors to the Wildfowl Trust show a special interest in these birds, and we now run a scheme so that people can support an individual swan. This income, of course, is much appreciated and helps to pay for the masses of wheat swans wolf their way through each week! If you would like to know more about this scheme, write to: The Wildfowl Trust, Slimbridge, Gloucestershire.

Helping Young Birds

Every summer you will find young birds which seem lost, deserted, or have fallen out of a nest and are unable to fend for themselves. What is the correct thing to do? The answer, 99 times out of 100, is **nothing**. Usually the birds are not lost or deserted, but are quite all right and simply waiting for the parents to come back with food.

A young bird may be cheeping away looking helpless (it is—it can't feed itself and it may not be able to fly) and hungry (it is—it wants the next meal which its parents will definitely not provide while you are hanging around). However, it is almost certainly not deserted, so the best thing is to **leave it alone** and let the parents get on with the job of feeding it—which they can do far better than you can. In nearly every case it is a mistaken kindness to 'rescue' a young bird and try to rear it yourself.

A possible exception to leaving a young bird alone is if you find one in a dangerous position, such as in the middle of the road. Pick it up carefully and take it to the verge where it is out of danger. Then quickly leave the scene, so that the parents can find it.

Only if you are absolutely certain that the bird is deserted and is unable to fend for itself (for instance, if you have seen the parents being killed by a cat) should you make any attempt to remove it and rear it yourself. Also, bear in mind that hand-rearing a young bird can be a very laborious and time-consuming business.

Remember that, in general, the best way of helping young birds is to leave them alone. Tell your friends this as well.

Oystercatchers

Birdwatchers' Calender

January

Wigeon, teal, tufted duck and pochard are all reaching peak numbers. More unusual wildfowl such as smew and goosander can be seen inland on reservoirs. Hard weather movements often bring in a rare bird. Very large flocks of knot, dunlin and oystercatchers on the coast. Finch flocks regularly hold bramblings. Birds of prey are seen in open spaces.

February

Very similar to January but more chance of an uncommon bird, or seabirds being seen inland. Unfrozen patches of water attract many species and your bird-table probably has its highest numbers this month. Most of the common birds begin to sing regularly again and crossbills start to nest.

Rooks

Crossbill

March

Larks and finches move to their breeding grounds, and rookeries are full of noise and bustle. Sand martins arrive to breed and winter visitors fly north to their nesting areas.

April

A busy month, as bird-watchers travel round to different habitats sighting the early arrivals and late departures. Most of the warblers return during this month, and as swallows, house martins, flycatchers and wheatears arrive, the last of the winter visitors depart. Large numbers of waders leave the coast and are regularly seen inland at sewage farms, reservoirs and lakes. Terns arrive to breed and the dawn chorus is improving daily.

Wigeon

John Markham

Pied Flycatcher

May

The last of the summer visitors, such as hobby, swift, nightjar and red-backed shrike arrive. Most of the breeding birds are now nesting and the first broods are fledged. This is an excellent month for locating woodland birds as there is so much song. Waders and terns are still passing through.

June

All the birds are busy with families; woods and hedgerows are worth searching for breeding surveys and records. Egrets and other oddities may be sighted as they 'overshoot' their normal migration routes. Not many flocks about, except perhaps the early and non-breeding birds.

July

A fairly dull month with late summer visitors still breeding and a slight trickle of non-breeding waders. Ruffs return in their winter plumage and common sandpipers pass through on passage.

J. B. & S. Bottomley (Ardea)

Black-tailed godwit

Fritz Polking (Bruce Coleman)

Hobby

Greenshank

Ake Lindau (Ardea)

August

Many waders are on the move and flocks are beginning to gather. Wood and curlew sandpipers and greenshank are seen. Terns are passing through and shearwaters are sighted offshore. Swifts start to leave.

S. C. Porter (Bruce Coleman)

Nightjar

September

The majority of summer visitors are now on the move, and early winter visitors are slowly starting to arrive. Bluethroats, wrynecks, red-breasted flycatchers and other rarities are seen down the east coast; a sea-watch is often very exciting. Little stints and American rarities lurk amongst the wader flocks. Watchers inland are often rewarded at sewage farms and other large expanses of water.

Hen Harrier

Wryneck

Fieldfare

October

Summer visitors are thin on the ground now. Redwings are common by the end of the month. Hawthorn and elder bushes often hold thrushes and are worth checking for fieldfares; it is worth looking on high ground for ring ouzels. Great grey-shrikes and waxwings arrive, and some finch flocks hold early bramblings. Snow buntings and shore larks are on the move again. Rarities, such as yellow-browed warbler and other Siberian birds may be recorded on the south and east coast; this is a good month for oddities.

November

Winter visitors are in flocks; geese and duck numbers are beginning to build up. More finch flocks are about and there are large numbers of tits. Birds are beginning to visit birdtables. Raptors such as peregrines, hen harriers, and merlins are more common.

December

Starlings are roosting in large numbers, and all the usual wintering birds are about. Winter waders are roosting in very large flocks and mute swans gather together in groups. Scoters, divers and other seaducks are increasing in numbers. Hard weather movements are sometimes interesting and raptors are well dispersed.

Eider Ducks

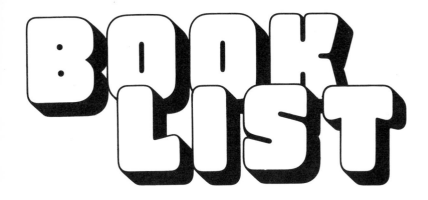

BOOK LIST

Deciding which bird books to buy can be difficult. So many books about birds are published that the choice can be bewildering. How do you start off?

For more than thirty years many people's first introduction to birdwatching was James Fisher's **Watching Birds**. It has recently been up-dated by Dr Jim Flegg. Some parts are a little difficult for younger readers to understand, but it contains much very useful information. An excellent background to a fascinating topic, it should be on every budding bird-watcher's bookshelf.

The first thing you will want to do, is to identify the birds that you see. There are two good titles which deal just with British birds – **The Observers' Book** and **The Oxford Book of Birds**. The first is small and fits into a pocket in your anorak, but each bird has a page to itself, whereas the Oxford book is large and each page carries a number of species.

There are three field guides dealing with British and European birds – **The Hamlyn Guide to Birds of Britain and Europe, A Field Guide to the Birds of Britain and Europe** and **Birds of Britain and Europe (with North Africa and the Middle East)**. All of them are well illustrated and arranged in a way that makes identification as easy as possible. But do beware – they cover many species that do not visit Britain – or are very rare.

A very good reference book that you can use at home is **The Popular Handbook of British Birds** by P A D Hollom. It contains information about food, places where birds live, and detailed descriptions of the birds.

Knowing about birds does not stop at being able to identify them. You also need to know what they are doing. A good introduction to the way they behave is **Birds** by Christopher Perrins. It is well written and explains as simply as possible why birds behave as they do. The **AA Book of Birds** has a section devoted to the whats and whys of birdlife. The first section of this book has some interesting information, but the illustrations, although very attractive, are rather misleading.

Bird Behaviour by John Sparks, **How Birds Behave** by Neil Ardley and **The Life of Birds** by Dr Maurice Burton are all well illustrated explanations of behaviour.

For the younger reader the Ladybird series of natural history and bird books are a marvellous introduction, with splendid illustrations and an easily understood text.

If you have good bird books you are well on the way to becoming a good birdwatcher, because, through good books, you will learn from the experience of the experts.

Watching Birds by James Fisher (Dr Jim Flegg), published by T and A D Poyser.

The Observer's Book of Birds published by Warne.

The Oxford Book of Birds published by OUP.

The Hamlyn Guide to Birds of Britain and Europe by Bruun and Singer, published by Hamlyn.

A Field Guide to the Birds of Britain and Europe by Peterson, Mountfort and Hollom, published by Collins.

Birds of Britain and Europe (with North Africa and the Middle East) by Heinzel, Fitter and Parslow, published by Collins.

The Popular Handbook of British Birds by P A D Hollom, published by Witherby.

Birds by Christopher Perrins, published by Collins.

AA Book of Birds

Bird Behaviour by John Sparks, published by Hamlyn.

How Birds Behave by Neil Ardley, published by Hamlyn.

The Life of Birds by Dr Maurice Burton, published by Macdonald.

Answers

Bird Puzzle

Nightingale, kingfisher, fieldfare, raven, wigeon, grey phalarope, golden eagle, wryneck, osprey, red grouse, kestrel, wren, jay, barn owl, heron, dunnock, avocet, greenfinch, coot, puffin, kite, knot, whinchat, cormorant, woodcock, twite, teal, smew, reeve and wood pigeon,

making 30 species in all.

Twenty Birds

The correct set of answers are:
Tawny owl, goldcrest, spotted flycatcher, tree creeper, greenfinch, pied wagtail, redshank, sand martin, rock pipit, marsh warbler, wood sandpiper (OR marsh sandpiper and wood warbler), little gull, common tern (OR little tern and common gull), hen harrier, corncrake, house sparrow, collared dove, reed bunting, black grouse and grey plover.

Bird Quiz

1. Swan; 2. Australia; 3. Crow; 4. Avocet; 5. Turkey; 6. Barnacle goose; 7. Robin, Blue tit, blackbird and black-headed gull; 8. No; 9. Wren; 10. Peacock.

PICTURE QUIZ

1. Long-tailed skua in flight; 2. Feet of a Coot standing on ice; 3. Black grouse; 4. Heron's neck; 5. Neck of Black-throated diver; 6. King eider; 7. Long-eared owl; 8. Head feathers of African hoopoe.